D0251172

DATE DUE

MAR 2 3 2004		
APR 1 7 2004		
OCT 0 7 2005		

Demco, Inc. 38-293

The Journey of
DESIRE

Searching for the
Life We've Only Dreamed Of

John Eldredge

Publishers Since 1798

THOMAS NELSON PUBLISHERS®
Nashville

A Division of Thomas Nelson, Inc.
www.ThomasNelson.com

Published in Nashville, Tennessee, by Thomas Nelson, Inc.

Published in association with Yates & Yates, LLP, Literary Agents, Orange, California.

Scripture quotations noted NIV are from the HOLY BIBLE: NEW INTERNATIONAL VERSION®. Copyright © 1973, 1978, 1984 by International Bible Society. Used by permission of Zondervan Publishing House. All rights reserved.

Scripture quotations noted NLT are from the *Holy Bible,* New Living Translation, copyright © 1996. Used by permission of Tyndale House Publishers, Inc., Wheaton, Illinois 60189. All rights reserved.

Scripture quotations noted *The Message* are from *The Message: The New Testament in Contemporary English.* Copyright © 1993 by Eugene H. Peterson.

Library of Congress Cataloging-in-Publication Data

Eldredge, John.
    The journey of desire: searching for the life we've only dreamed of / John Eldredge.
        p. cm.
    ISBN 0-7852-6882-0 (hc)
    1. Christian life. 2. Desire—Religious aspects—Christianity. I. Title.
BV4501.2.E343 2000
248.4—dc21

99-059021
CIP

Printed in the United States of America.
26 BVG 06 05 04 03

For Brent

CONTENTS

I did not intend to write this book alone. Brent Curtis, with whom I wrote *The Sacred Romance*, was a marvelous coauthor and I had looked forward to many years of working together. Indeed, all of my visions for the future included him, for he was my dearest friend. But as you shall soon discover in these pages, Brent was killed in May of '98. I have struggled to even speak of it, partly in fear that these thoughts will be dismissed as the ruminations of a grieving man. But this book had already been several years in the making, in that I had been taking notes on the subject for some time. I have long believed that the journey of desire is the central journey of the soul. But after Brent's death, writing became a necessity. The truths contained here suddenly became all the *more* true.

Still, I did not write entirely alone. As Pascal reminds us in his *Pensées*, "Some authors, when talking of their works, say, *my* book, *my* commentary, *my* history, etc. I recommend them to say, *our* book, because in general they contain much more of what belongs to other people than to themselves." How right he is. I readily confess the influence of so many—my family and friends, my clients and the authors that I love. No doubt you will find many of their thoughts here. I only wish I could personally thank each of them. In hopes that they will understand something of my gratitude, I will risk naming but a few of the men and women to whom I am indebted.

To Rolf Zettersten, Publisher of Thomas Nelson Books: Thank you for phoning one afternoon to ask if I would ever write again.

To Brian Hampton, my editor: The thought of working with a new editor was not a welcome one to me, but you have more than allayed my fears. Your understanding and skill have meant a great deal to me in the realization of this work.

To Sealy Yates: I am deeply grateful for all your wisdom and counsel. You are more than an agent par excellence—you are a man of deep desire.

To Mike Rosebush: Your gracious leadership has allowed this book to become a reality. Thanks for all your support.

To Bart Hansen: Neither of us had any idea what was to unfold at the ranch that fateful afternoon. How can I ever thank you for standing with me through those agonizing days and months, for your encouragement and for your friendship?

To Gary, Leigh, and Joni: You are more than friends; you are *allies*. Stasi and I are richer people for having you in our lives.

To Jan: For walking the journey with us, for keeping your own heart alive, for living with such gracious courage, you have strengthened me. And your reaction to the manuscript was more than I could have asked for. Thank you.

To Stasi, my wife: Your enthusiasm was, above all else, my source of inspiration to press on. The thing about writing is, I have no idea if what I'm saying is any good. I'm far too close to it. This was especially so with *The Journey of Desire*, which I was destined to write in the solitary confinement of the basement. Your wonderful responses to the unfolding chapters were like cold water to a very thirsty man. You love me well.

To my sons, Samuel, Blaine, and Luke: Thanks for letting Dad disappear downstairs so many nights. And thanks for sneaking down to remind me that it was time to stop and play. I love to write, but I love you more. Let's go wrestle.

To all the dear friends who have been praying for me: None of this would have happened without you. You know what a spiritual Vietnam this has been; thank you seems far too inadequate for providing such cover.

Finally, my deepest thanks to the men and women who have shared with me their own journeys of desire: I am honored to be called your friend. This truly is *our* book.

The Journey of
DESIRE

———

Once upon a time there lived a sea lion who had lost the sea.

He lived in a country known as the barren lands. High on a plateau, far from any coast, it was a place so dry and dusty that it could only be called a desert. A kind of coarse grass grew in patches here and there, and a few trees were scattered across the horizon. But mostly, it was dust. And sometimes wind, which together make one very thirsty. Of course, it must seem strange to you that such a beautiful creature should wind up in a desert at all. He was, mind you, a sea lion. But things like this do happen.

How the sea lion came to the barren lands, no one could remember. It all seemed so very long ago. So long, in fact, it appeared as though he had always been there. Not that he belonged in such an arid place. How could that be? He was, after all, a sea lion. But as you know, once you have lived so long in a certain spot, no matter how odd, you come to think of it as home.

———

CHAPTER ONE

OUR HEART'S DEEPEST SECRET

We are never living, but hoping to live.

—Pascal

It seems to me we can never give up longing and wishing while we are alive. There are certain things we feel to be beautiful and good, and we must hunger for them.

—George Eliot

And I still haven't found what I'm looking for.

—U2

There is a secret set within each of our hearts. It often goes unnoticed, we rarely can put words to it, and yet it guides us throughout the days of our lives. This secret remains hidden for the most part in our deepest selves. It is the desire for life as it was meant to be. Isn't there a life you have been searching for all your days? You may not always be aware of your search, and there are times when you seem to have abandoned looking altogether. But again and again it returns to us, this yearning that cries out for the life we prize. It is elusive, to be sure. It seems to come and go at will. Seasons may pass until it surfaces again. And though it seems to taunt us, and may at times cause us great pain, we know when it returns that it is priceless. For if we could recover this desire, unearth it from beneath all other distractions, and embrace it as our deepest treasure, we would discover the secret of our existence.

You see, life comes to all of us as a mystery. We all share the same dilemma—we long for life and we're not sure where to find it. We wonder if we ever do find it, can we make it last? The longing for life within us seems incongruent with the life we find around us. What is available seems at times close to what we want, but never quite a fit. Our days come to us as a riddle, and the answers aren't handed out with our birth certificates. We must journey to find the life we prize. And the guide we have been given is the desire set deep within, the desire we often overlook or mistake for something else or even choose to ignore.

The greatest human tragedy is to give up the search. Nothing is of greater importance than the life of our deep heart. To lose heart is to lose everything. And if we are to bring our hearts along in our life's journey, we simply must not, we cannot, abandon this desire. Gerald May writes in *The Awakened Heart,*

> There is a desire within each of us, in the deep center of ourselves that we call our heart. We were born with it, it is never completely satisfied, and it never dies. We are often unaware of it, but it is always awake . . . Our true identity, our reason for being, is to be found in this desire.

The clue as to who we really are and why we are here comes to us through our heart's desire. But it comes in surprising ways, and often goes unnoticed or is misunderstood. Once in a while life comes together for us in a way that feels good and right and what we've been waiting for. These are the moments in our lives that we wish could go on forever. They aren't necessarily the

"Kodak moments," weddings and births and great achievements. More often than not they come in subtler, unexpected ways, as if to sneak up on us.

Think of times in your life that made you wish for all the world that you had the power to make time stand still. Are they not moments of love, moments of joy? Simple moments of rest and quiet when all seems to be well. Something in your heart says, *Finally—it has come. This is what I was made for!*

WHISPERS OF JOY

It was the final evening of our summer vacation. We had spent nine wonderful days in the Tetons hiking and swimming, laughing and playing, enjoying rare and wonderful time together as a family in a stunningly beautiful place. During our explorations, we had discovered a quiet pond in the woods, about a half hour's walk from camp, where wildlife would often come in the evening. This night, we planned to arrive at dusk and stay until night fell to see what nature might reveal. The sun was setting behind us as we arrived, and far off in the east massive thunderheads were building above the Absarokas, cloud upon cloud, giant castles in the sky. The fading day was slowly turning them peach, then pink, then gray.

A pair of trumpeter swans were swimming across our little pond, looking for all the world like something from a fairy tale. My wife and I sat together with our three boys on a spot of grass near the water's edge, our backs against a fallen log. Across the pond lay a meadow, the stage for the evening's drama. As light began to fade, a bull moose with a massive rack emerged from the willows directly across the meadow from where we sat. He spotted us and stopped; we held our breath. Silently, he disappeared into the trees as mysteriously as he had come. Before we could be disappointed, a cow moose and her calf appeared from another part of the meadow, wandering along grazing. We watched them as night continued to fall.

A cool breeze stirred the pines above us. Crickets began their twilight chorus. The cow lay down in the tall grass, but we could still see her calf. Sandhill cranes were calling and answering one another around the marsh with their haunting, primeval cries. The boys huddled closer to us. A beaver swam by our feet, making a V through the surface of the pond, faded with the light to a gunmetal gray. Far off in the distance, lightning was beginning within those cloud fortresses, flashes of glory. A small herd of elk came out to graze at the far end of the meadow, just as darkness was settling in. Finally, as if not to be left out, a lone coyote began to howl. It was one of the most breathtaking nights I have ever experienced in the wilderness, a living work of art. As the Scottish poet George MacDonald knew so well, something is calling to us in moments like these.

> Yet hints come to me from the realm unknown;
> Airs drift across the twilight border land,
> Odored with life;
> . . . whispers to my heart are blown
> That fill me with a joy I cannot speak,
> Yea, from whose shadow words drop faint and weak.
>
> (*Diary of an Old Soul*)

I know these years are passing quickly, and the time will come when our boys will no longer want to vacation with us. They will find other loves and form other ties, and our lives will never be the same again. Sitting there with them in the woods, clutching their flashlights, whispering to each other about each passing mystery, I would have given anything to stop the clock, turn it back if only for a few days, let us live it all again. But the seasons pass with or without our permission, and I knew in my heart we could not stay. For a moment, we were all caught up in something bigger and more beautiful than we had ever known, "suspended above the earth," as Norman MacLean says, "free from all its laws, like a work of art. And I knew just as surely and just as clearly, that life is not a work of art, and that the moment could not last."

ECHOES FROM THE PAST

Sometimes these moments go unrecognized as they unfold, but their secret comes to us years later in our longing to relive them. Aren't there times in your life that if you could, you would love to return to? I grew up in Los Angeles but spent my boyhood summers in Oregon where both my mother's and my father's parents lived. There was a beauty and innocence and excitement to those days. Woods to explore, rivers to fish, grandparents to fuss over me. My parents were young and in love, and the days were full of adventures I did not have to create or pay for, but only live in and enjoy. Rafting and swimming in the Rogue River. Playing in the park. Huckleberry pie at Becky's along the road to Crater Lake. We all have places in our past when life, if only for a moment, seemed to be coming together in the way we knew in our hearts it was always meant to be.

There was a time when meadow, grove, and stream,
The earth, and every common sight,
To me did seem
Appareled in celestial light,
The glory and the freshness of a dream . . .
Heaven lies about us in our infancy;

5

Shades of the prison-house begin to close
Upon the growing boy,
But he beholds the light, and whence it flows.
He sees it in his joy; . . .
At length the man perceives it die away,
And fade into the light of common day.
(*Ode, Intimations of Immortality from Recollection of Childhood*)

Wordsworth caught a glimpse of the secret in his childhood, saw in it hints from the realm unknown. We must learn the lesson of these moments, or we will not be able to bring our hearts along in our life's journey. For if these moments pass, never to be recovered again, then the life we prize is always fading from view, and our hearts with it. It isn't until the kids are out of the house that you realize how precious were those years. The inflatable pool in the backyard. The stockings hung up at Christmastime. First steps and first home runs and first dates. We fill photo albums with all these moments, trying to hang on to them somehow. We hate to see them slip away. Our losses seem to say that the life we prize will never be ours, never come to stay. But the secret is coming to us even in our greatest losses.

SHOUTS OF LAMENT

I did not know how much Brent meant to me until I lost him. He was killed last year at this time, in a climbing accident. We had taken a group of men to the mountains on a retreat, believing that to help a man recover his heart, you must take him out of the office, away from the television, and into the wild. We planned three days at a ranch in Colorado where we would bring rock climbing, fly-fishing, and horseback riding together with talks on the journey of a man's heart. Brent was leading the climbing on day two when he fell. The loss was unspeakable for many, many people. Ginny lost her husband. Ben and Drew lost their daddy. Many people lost the only man who had ever fought for their hearts.

I lost the truest friend I have ever known. Brent was more than my partner; he was for me the rarest of gifts—his heart saw what mine saw. Our friendship was a shared journey, a mutual quest, for the secret of our souls. It took us into the mountains, into literature and music, into the desperate battle raging all around for the hearts of others as well. We laughed and grieved and scorned and yearned all along the way. When he lost his son in a mountaineering accident, Nicholas Wolterstorff wrote,

> There's a hole in the world now . . . A center, like no other, of memory and hope and knowledge and affection which once inhabited this earth is gone. Only a gap remains. A perspective in this world unique in this world which once moved about in this world has been rubbed out . . . There's nobody who saw just what he saw, knows what he knew, remembers what he remembered, loves what he loved . . . Questions I have can never now get answers. The world is emptier. (*Lament for a Son*)

This is silly, really, and a little embarrassing, but I find myself turning suddenly when I see a silver gray Jeep pass by. I look to see if it is his, if he is there. Brent is gone; I know that. How I know that. But still, I find myself doing a double take when I see a Jeep like his. Something rises in me, something beyond reason. A hope that perhaps it is his, that he is driving past me again. The other day I was in a parking lot and saw a beat-up old Cherokee with a rack on top. I stopped, went over, and looked. I know in my head that this is ridiculous. Brent is gone. But my heart refuses at some level to accept it. Or rather, my yearning for things to be right is so strong that it overrides my logic and turns my head, in hope against hope, every time.

"The heart," Blaise Pascal said, "has its reasons which reason knows not of." Something in us longs, hopes, maybe even at times believes that this is not the way things were supposed to be. Our desire fights the assault of death upon life. And so people with terminal illnesses get married. Prisoners in a concentration camp plant flowers. Lovers long divorced still reach out in the night to embrace one who is no longer there. It's like the phantom pain experienced by those who have lost a limb. Feelings still emanate from that region where once was a crucial part of them, and they will sometimes find themselves being careful not to bang the corner of a table or slam the car door on a leg or an arm long since removed. Our hearts know a similar reality. At some deep level, we refuse to accept the fact that this is the way things are, or must be, or always will be.

Simone Weil was right; there are only two things that pierce the human heart: beauty and affliction. Moments we wish would last forever and moments we wish had never begun. What are we to make of these messengers? How are we to interpret what they are saying? The playwright Christopher Fry writes,

> The inescapable dramatic situation for us all is that we have no idea what our situation is. We may be mortal. What then? We may be immortal. What then? We are plunged into an existence fantastic to the point of nightmare, and however hard we rationalize, or however firm our religious faith, however closely we dog the heels of science or wheel among the starts of mysticism, we cannot really make head or tail of it. ("A Playwright Speaks: How Lost, How Amazed, How Miraculous We Are")

And what does Fry say we do with our dilemma? The worst of all possible reactions:

We get used to it. We get broken into it so gradually we scarcely notice it.

THE SAME OLD THING

Something awful has happened; something terrible. Something worse, even, than the fall of man. For in that greatest of all tragedies, we merely lost Paradise—and with it, everything that made life worth living. What has happened since is unthinkable: we've gotten used to it. We're broken in to the idea that this is just the way things are. The people who walk in great darkness have adjusted their eyes. Regardless of our religious or philosophical beliefs, most of us live as though this life is pretty much the way things are supposed to be. We dismiss the whispers of joy with a cynical "Been there, done that, bought the T-shirt." That way we won't have to deal with the haunting.

I was just talking with some friends about summer vacations, and I recommended that they visit the Tetons. "Oh, yeah, we've been there. Nice place." Dismissal. And we deaden our sorrows with cynicism as well, sporting a bumper sticker that says, "Life sucks. Then you die." Then we try to get on with life. We feed the cat, pay the bills, watch the news, and head off to bed, so we can do it all again tomorrow.

Standing before the open fridge, I'm struck by what I've just watched. Famine in Africa. Genocide . . . where? Someplace I can't even pronounce. I think it used to be part of the Soviet bloc. Corruption in Washington. Life as usual. It always ends with the anchor folding his notes and offering a pleasant "Good night." Good night? That's it? You have nothing else to say? You've just regaled us with the horrors of the world we live in, and all you can say is "Good night"? To be fair, he did promise more details—with film—at eleven. Just once I wish he would pause at the close of his report, take a long, deep breath, and then say, "How far we are from home," or "If only we had listened," or "Thank God, our sojourn here is drawing to an end." It never happens. I doubt it ever will. And not one of us gives it a second thought. It's just the way things are. Anytime I ask my neighbor how life is going, he always replies, "Same old thing."

Think with me for a moment. How has life turned out differently from the way you thought it would? If you are single, did you want to be? If you are married, is this the marriage you hoped for? Do you long to have children, or in having them, are you delighted with the course they've chosen for their lives? Your friendships—are they as rich and deep and lasting as you want? When the holidays roll around, do you look forward with eager anticipation to the time you'll spend with the people in your life? And afterward, as you pack away the decorations and clean up the mess, did the reality match your expectations?

How about your work, your place in the world—do you go to bed each night with a deep sense of having made a lasting contribution? Do you enjoy ongoing recognition for your unique successes? Are you even working in a field that fits you? Are you working at all? Now, what if I told you that this is how it will always be, that this life as you now experience it will go on forever just as it is, without improvement of any kind? Your health will stay as it is; your finances will remain as they are, your relationships, your work, all of it.

It is hell.

IN DEFENSE OF DISCONTENT

By the grace of God, we cannot quite pull it off. In the quiet moments of the day we sense a nagging within, a discontent, a hunger for something else. But because we have not solved the riddle of our existence, we assume that something is wrong—not with life, but with us. *Everyone else seems to be getting on with things. What's wrong with me?* We feel guilty about our chronic disappointment. *Why can't I just learn to be happier in my job, in my marriage, in my church, in my group of friends?* You see, even while we are doing other things, "getting on with life," we still have an eye out for the life we secretly want. When someone seems to have gotten it together, we wonder, *How did he do it?* Maybe if we read the same book, spent time with him, went to his church, things would come together for us as well. We can never entirely give up our quest. May reminds us,

> When the desire is too much to bear, we often bury it beneath frenzied thoughts and activities or escape it by dulling our immediate consciousness of living. It is possible to run away from the desire for years, even decades, at a time, but we cannot eradicate it entirely. It keeps touching us in little glimpses and hints in our dreams, our hopes, our unguarded moments. (*The Awakened Heart*)

He says that even though we sleep, our desire does not. "It is who we are." We *are* desire. It is the essence of the human soul, the secret of our existence. Absolutely nothing of human greatness is ever accomplished without it. Not a symphony has been written, a mountain climbed, an injustice fought, or a love sustained apart from desire. Desire fuels our search for the life we prize. Our desire, if we will listen to it, will save us from committing soul-suicide, the sacrifice of our hearts on the altar of "getting by." The same old thing is not enough. It never will be.

The secret that begins to solve the riddle of our lives is simply this: we are the sea lion who lost the sea. Life as usual is not the life we truly want. It is not the life we truly need. It is not the life we were made for. If we would only listen to our hearts, to what G. K. Chesterton called our "divine discontent," we would learn the secret of our existence. As he wrote in *Orthodoxy*, "We have come to the wrong star . . . That is what makes life at once so splendid and so strange. The true happiness is that we *don't* fit. We come from somewhere else. We have lost our way."

The meaning of our lives is revealed through experiences that at first seem at odds with each other—moments we wish would never end and moments we wish had never begun. Those timeless experiences we want to last forever whisper to us that *they were meant to*. We were made to live in a world of beauty and wonder, intimacy and adventure all our days. Nathaniel Hawthorne insisted, "Our Creator would never have made such lovely days, and given us the deep hearts to enjoy them, above and beyond all thought, unless we were meant to be immortal."

There is more to these days than pictures tucked away in photo albums, fading as the memory fades from view. We use a statement to try to console ourselves with what we think is the irrecoverable loss: "All good things come to an end." I hate that phrase. It's a lie. Even our troubles and our heartbreaks tell us something about our true destiny. The tragedies that strike us to the core and elicit the cry, "This isn't the way it was supposed to be!" are also telling the truth—it *isn't* the way it was supposed to be. Pascal writes,

> Man is so great that his greatness appears even in knowing himself to be miserable. A tree has no sense of its misery. It is true that to know we are miserable is to be miserable; but to know we are miserable is also to be great. Thus all the miseries of man prove his grandeur; they are the miseries of a dignified personage, the miseries of a dethroned monarch . . . What can this incessant craving, and this impotence of attainment mean, unless there was once a

happiness belonging to man, of which only the faintest traces remain, in that void which he attempts to fill with everything within his reach? *(Pensées)*

Should the king in exile pretend he is happy there? Should he not seek his own country? His miseries are his ally; they urge him on. Let them grow, if need be. But do not forsake the secret of life; do not despise those kingly desires. We abandon the most important journey of our lives when we abandon desire. We leave our hearts by the side of the road and head off in the direction of fitting in, getting by, being productive, what have you. Whatever we might gain—money, position, the approval of others, or just absence of the discontent itself—it's not worth it. "What good will it be for a man if he gains the whole world, yet forfeits his soul?" (Matt. 16:26 NIV).

TAKING UP THE QUEST

We must return to the journey. Wherever we are, whatever we are doing, we must pick up the trail and follow the map that we have at hand. Desire, both the whispers and the shouts, is the map we have been given to find the only life worth living. You may think you are following the map of desire when all you are doing is serving it slavishly, unthinkingly. It is not the same. We must *listen* to desire, look at it carefully, let it guide us through the false routes and dead ends. C. S. Lewis advises us,

> I knew only too well how easily the longing accepts false objects and through what dark ways the pursuit of them leads us. But I also saw that the Desire itself contains the corrective of all these errors. The only fatal error was to pretend you had passed from desire to fruition, when, in

reality, you had found either nothing, or desire itself, or the satisfaction of some different desire. The dialectic of Desire, faithfully followed, would retrieve all mistakes, head you off from all false paths, and force you to live through . . . a sort of [experiential] proof. (*The Pilgrim's Regress*)

The only fatal error is to pretend that we have found the life we prize. To mistake the water hole for the sea. To settle for the same old thing. Fry called such a life "the sleep of prisoners." You might remember the movie *The Shawshank Redemption*, the story of prison life in the Northeast in the 1940s. The film focuses on the journey of two men's hearts through the trials and temptations of incarceration. Red, the ringleader and most seasoned of the prisoners, explains what happens when you live within those walls too long: "At first, these walls, you hate them. They make you crazy. After a while you get used to 'em, don't notice 'em anymore. Then comes the day you realize you need them." That is the most tragic day of all—to prefer slavery to freedom, to prefer death to life. We must not stay in this sleep. The time has come for us to wake, to arise from our slumber. As the Scriptures say, "Wake up, O sleeper, rise from the dead" (Eph. 5:14 NIV). And so MacDonald prayed,

> When I can no more stir my soul to move,
> And life is but the ashes of a fire;
> When I can but remember that my heart
> Once used to live and love, long and aspire—
> Oh, be thou then the first, the one thou art;
> Be thou the calling, before all answering love,
> And in me wake hope, fear, boundless desire.
> (*Diary of an Old Soul*)

Bringing our heart along in our life's journey is the most important mission of our lives—and the hardest. It all turns on what we do with our desire. If you will look around, you will see that most people have abandoned the journey. They have lost heart. They are camped in places of resignation or indulgence, or trapped in prisons of despair. I understand; I have frequented all those places before and return to them even still. Life provides any number of reasons and occasions to abandon desire. Certainly, one of the primary reasons is that it creates for us our deepest dilemmas. To desire something and not to have it—is this not the source of nearly all our pain and sorrow?

There was a time, many years back, when the sea lion knew he was lost. In those days, he would stop every traveler he met to see if he might help him find his way back to the sea.

But no one seemed to know the way.

On he searched, but never finding. After years without success, the sea lion took refuge beneath a solitary tree beside a very small water hole. The tree provided refuge from the burning rays of the sun, which was very fierce in that place. And the water hole, though small and muddy, was wet, in its own way. Here he settled down and got on as best he could.

CHAPTER TWO

THE DILEMMA
OF DESIRE

I never knew the dusk could break my heart
So much longing folding in
I'd give years away to have you here
To know I can't lose you again.

—Fernando Ortega

Who needs a heart when a heart can be broken?

—Tina Turner

I am almost committing an indecency. I am trying to rip open
the inconsolable secret in each one of you—the secret which
hurts so much that you take your revenge on it by calling it
names like Nostalgia and Romanticism and Adolescence.

—C. S. Lewis

High on the slopes of the world's tallest mountain, slightly less than twenty-nine thousand feet above the level of the sea, the climber has halted in his tracks. He can go no farther. His whole life has come down to this. After years of planning and preparation, he has trekked halfway across the globe to a strange country high in the Himalayas. He has drained his bank account and damaged his relationships. His career has suffered. He has sacrificed everything in his life for this moment. But none of that matters now. He is exhausted. His breathing is labored. He is forced to pause after each step for three heaving breaths, followed by another step, then a pause. As he creeps along a razor's edge of snow, each move requires an agonizing amount of concentration. Oxygen deprivation reduces his mental faculties to those of a small child. Ahead of him rises the Hillary Step, a forty-foot wall of nearly vertical ice. It is all that stands between him and the goal of his life. But he is not sure he can go on.

I am haunted by the stories of people who make the summit of Everest. Such incredible devotion is required, such total focus of body, soul, and spirit. Reaching the top of the world's tallest mountain becomes for those who try the central driving force of their lives. The goal is remarkable and the journey uncertain. Many climbers have been lost on the mountain. Those who reach the summit and return safely are among a rare and elite group of mountaineers in the world. Why do they do it? *How* do they do it?

Jon Krakauer recounted the desperate tale of the ill-fated '96 expedition in his book *Into Thin Air:* "There were many, many fine reasons not to go, but attempting to climb Everest is an intrinsically irrational act—a triumph of desire over sensibility." It is a feat begun in desire that can be accomplished only through desire. Krakauer explained how one of his climbing partners attained the summit: "Yasuko had been propelled up the mountain by the unwavering intensity of her desire."

Desire—it's the only way you will ever make it. Take marriage, for instance. Or singleness. Either makes for a far more difficult and arduous ascent than Everest, in large part because it does not seem so. The struggles are not heightened and focused into one month of do or die; rather, they stretch on across a lifetime. So it is with any act of faith or of hope—anything, in other words, that makes a life worth living. How can we possibly sustain such an intrinsically irrational act as love if we've killed our desire? May honestly admits,

> Choosing love will open spaces of immense beauty and joy for you, but you will be hurt. You already know this. You have retreated from love countless times in your life because of it. We all have. We have been and will be hurt by the loss of loved ones, by what they have done to us and we to them. Even in the bliss of love there is a certain exquisite pain: the pain of too much beauty, of overwhelming magnificence. Further, no matter how perfect a love may be, it is never really satisfied . . . In both joy and pain, love is boundless. (*The Awakened Heart*)

Desire is the source of our most noble aspirations and our deepest sorrows. The pleasure and the pain go together; indeed, they emanate from the same region in our hearts. We cannot live without the yearning, and yet the yearning sets us up for disappointment—sometimes deep and devastating disappointment. One storm claimed the lives of eight of Krakauer's companions in the Everest disaster of 1996. Should they not have tried? Many have said they were foolish even to begin. Do we reach for nothing in life because our reaching opens us up to tragedy? Because of its vulnerable nature, desire begins to feel like our worst enemy.

FRIEND OR FOE?

"I'm beginning to despise the hope." We were talking about life, a friend and I, and how hard it was to keep pressing on. David had been through a series of setbacks in his career, going from earning a six-figure income at a top Wall Street firm to driving a courier van, making deliveries. It's the hardest fall a man takes. He didn't want to be there; he wanted to climb out of the slump he was in. Occasionally, an opportunity would present itself. He'd get a call or a contact through a friend. Putting on a coat and tie, David would head out into the arena. The desire for something better would resurface, only to be thwarted. The interview seemed to go well at the time, but then he'd sit by the phone and the call would never come. Each time he reached for a rung up the ladder, the rung broke, and he found himself back at the bottom. After several years of the cycle, he found himself despising hope. "It just sets me up for another fall. Why bother?"

I think of another friend, Carol, whose life has been marked over the years by one disappointing relationship after another. Just when she is ready to call it quits on loving altogether, hope appears on the horizon. She ventures out cautiously. And several months later, her heart is broken again. Over lunch yesterday she used nearly the same words: "I hate hope." Hope rouses the desire from its slumber and makes us even more vulnerable to disappointment.

As Carol and I spoke about life and love, I thought of Fantine, one of the tragic characters in Victor Hugo's novel *Les Misérables*. Fantine is a young single mother who works in a factory to support her daughter, whom she had to send away to live with an innkeeper. Fired for refusing the sexual advances of the foreman, she finds herself on the streets without a job, a place to stay, or a means of caring for her child. Those of you who have seen the musical will recall the hauntingly beautiful song she sings, entitled "I Dreamed a Dream."

> I had a dream in time gone by
> When hope was high

> And life worth living
> I dreamed that love would never die
> I dreamed that God would be forgiving

She remembers being young and unafraid, that time in our lives when dreams are "made and used and wasted." She tells of a love that came to her, filling her days with endless wonder. He became the father of her child and then, one day, disappeared. She dreams he will return, but knows he never will. I know too many women who have lived through this nightmare. Their lives are filled with weariness, loneliness, and resignation. Fantine ends by singing,

> I had a dream my life would be
> So different from this hell I'm living
> So different now from what it seemed
> Now life has killed the dream I dreamed.

WHEN DREAMS DIE

I understand. I know the dilemma of desire. Brent was killed on the doorstep of our dreams. You see, as our friendship deepened over the years, we discovered within us a similar hope. Long before I met him, I had begun to dream of having a ranch where people could come to recover their hearts, a place of beauty and adventure where one could learn about life's journey. I was shy to even mention it; heaven knows I had hidden it from everyone for years. How stunned with delight I was to find that he held the same desire. C. S. Lewis knew:

Are not all lifelong friendships born at the moment when at last you meet another human being who has some inkling . . .

of that something which you were born desiring, and which, beneath the flux of other desires and in all the momentary silences between the louder passions, night and day, year by year, from childhood to old age, you are looking for, watching for, listening for? (*The Problem of Pain*)

God seemed to be affirming that dream as we partnered together, speaking at conferences, writing, counseling. Still, it felt like courage even to allow ourselves to dream. We had both known enough disappointment in our lives to be wary of hope; maybe we'd both grown more than a little resigned. Both of us had been failed deeply by key men in our lives. Dare we trust?

Yet something deeper in us urged us to move forward. Alexander Pope knew that "hope springs eternal in the human breast." We planned to begin this great ascent of our desire last May, inviting a small group of men to join us on a ranch for a long weekend of conversation and adventure. It would be the inaugural voyage, the test flight for our dream. On the afternoon of the second day, Brent was killed. The rocks on which he was standing eighty feet above the ground crumbled beneath him.

"Despair," wrote James Houston, "is the fate of the desiring soul." Or as Scripture says, "Hope deferred makes the heart sick" (Prov. 13:12 NLT). How agonizing it can be to awaken desire! Over the past year I have wrestled deeply with what it means to go on. God has come to me again and again, insisting that I not give up the dream. I have ranted and railed, fought him and dismissed him. It feels crazy to desire anymore. What does it mean to live the rest of my life without my closest friend? I think of Lewis and Clark, those inseparable wilderness explorers, how we cannot think of one without the other. Lewis said of his companion, "I could neither hope, wish, nor expect from a union with any man on earth, more perfect support or further aid in the discharge of my mission, than that, which I am confident I shall derive from being associated with yourself." I know I shall never find another like him.

But I am not alone in this. Most of you will by this time have lost a parent, a spouse, even a child. Your hopes for your career have not panned out. Your health has given way. Relationships have turned sour. We all know the dilemma of desire, how awful it feels to open our hearts to joy, only to have grief come in. They go together. We know that. What we don't know is what to do with it, how to live in this world with desire so deep in us and disappointment lurking behind every corner. After we've taken a few arrows, dare we even desire?

I have come to the point that I am able to start looking at ranches again, but I can barely open myself to friendship. Still, something in me knows that to kill desire is to kill my heart altogether. Langston Hughes wrote,

> Hold fast to dreams
> For if dreams die
> Life is a broken-winged bird
> That cannot fly.
> Hold fast to dreams
> For when dreams go
> Life is a barren field
> Frozen with snow. ("Dreams")

Do we form no friendships because our friends might be taken from us? Do we refuse to love because we may be hurt? Do we forsake our dreams because hope has been deferred? To desire is to open our hearts to the possibility of pain; to shut down our hearts is to die altogether. The full proverb reads this way:

"Hope deferred makes the heart sick, *but when dreams come true, there is life and joy.*"

The road to life and joy lies through, not around, the heart-sickness of hope deferred. A good friend came to this realization recently. As we sat talking over breakfast, he put words to our dilemma: "I stand at the crossroads, and I am afraid of the desire. For forty-one years I've tried to control my life by killing the desire, but I can't. Now I know it. But to allow it to be, to let it out is frightening because I know I'll have to give up the control of my life. Is there another option?"

The option most of us have chosen is to reduce our desire to a more manageable size. We allow it out only in small doses—just what we can arrange for. Dinner out, a new sofa, a vacation to look forward to, a little too much to drink. It's not working. The tremors of the earthquake inside are beginning to break out.

THE BATTLE BETWEEN US

I haven't been the friendliest driver lately. Oh, I'm fine—until I'm provoked. When people cut me off, I'm furious. Just the other day, a car began to get on the highway as I was passing by. The fellow ignored all the rules of merging and cut in front of me as I was doing full speed. I hit my brakes to avoid him and honked my horn. He looked back, snarled, and yelled something unprintable. That did it. Only the fear of higher insurance premiums kept me from running him off the road. But oh, how I wanted to. Of course, this never happens to you. You are kind and benevolent when someone cuts you off. Why, you're practically happy when he steals your parking place, darts in right ahead of you. You smile and offer a blessing.

What is causing the quarrels and fights among you? Isn't it the whole army of evil desires at war within you? You want what you don't have, so you scheme and kill to get it. You are jealous for what others have, and you can't possess it, so you fight and quarrel to take it away from them. (James 4:1–2 NLT)

What do you make of all the road rage that's been surfacing? You don't think it's really about traffic etiquette, do you? People are shooting at each other on the freeway. This is not about bad manners or a need for driver's ed. There is something deeper, something pent up inside us. The fellow who cut me off didn't really endanger my life; but the violation felt like a symbol of a deeper, ongoing reality. Dan Allender points out,

> In every person there is a passionate, driving desire for more . . . The dilemma is that our longings for material joy are almost always partially blocked; our desires for better health and deeper relationships are never entirely possible; and the illusion of world peace seems no more attainable than the gold at the end of the rainbow. Our passion is more than usually stymied. The world simply does not bend to the desires that roar or whimper inside us. Our desires—from picking the quickest line at the bank to the overwhelming hope that our children will walk righteously with the Lord—are rarely satisfied in a way that relieves the ache of incompleteness . . . Our heart seems to rage against the ache. Our typical response to the heartbreak and sorrow of disappointment is murderous rage . . . We want someone to pay. (*Bold Love*)

The life we have is so far from the life we truly want, and it doesn't take us long to find someone to blame. In order for our longings to be filled, we need the cooperation of others. I long for a loving embrace and a kind word when I get home. I long for my boys to listen attentively when I talk about important life lessons. I want my work to be appreciated. I want my friends to be there for me in hard times. "No man is an island," wrote John Donne, and he could have been speaking of desire. We need others—it's part of our design. Very few of our desires are self-fulfilling; *all* our deepest longings require others to come through for us. Inevitably, someone stands in the way.

At its best, the world is indifferent to my desires. The air traffic controllers aren't the least affected when I've been traveling for a week and the plane they've chosen to cancel is my last chance to get home to my family. So long as it doesn't affect them, they couldn't care less. We suffer the violation of indifference on a daily basis, from friends, from family, from complete strangers. We think we've grown to accept it as part of life, but the effect is building inside us. We weren't made to be ignored. And though we try to pretend it doesn't really matter, the collective effect of living in a world apathetic to our existence is doing damage to our souls. Events such as bad traffic or delayed flights are merely the *occasions* for our true desperation to come out. As our desires come into direct conflict with the desires of another person, things get downright hostile.

We fought the Gulf War because Saddam Hussein wanted the rich oil fields of Kuwait. Phil and Diane fought the bedroom war over pork chops. They had invited another couple for dinner, and as Diane went out for the afternoon, she asked Phil to get the pork chops out of the freezer to thaw. He was working on the lawn mower and forgot. Dinnertime arrived, and Diane asked Phil to put the chops on the grill. He suddenly remembered that they were still hard as rocks in the freezer. You know the phrase "if looks could kill"? Diane couldn't say what she wanted to say. Their guests were sitting right there, and she had an image to maintain. She let Phil have it with a look and later that night finished the job off when they were alone.

Søren Kierkegaard said that resentment is the "constituent principle" of the modern era, this simmering anger at our blocked desires. We shove them beneath the surface for as long as possible, only to have them erupt on the freeway, in the class-room, or at home in a burst of physical or verbal retaliation. Our anger is rarely proportionate to the event. I yelled at my five-year-old son, Luke, at dinner tonight because he was being dis-respectful to his mom. But is that all that was behind my stern rebuke? Aren't events like that the triggers, opening the doors to a reservoir of disappointment we pretend for the most part we have risen above? We try to get beyond the pain of desire by burying it, but it does not go away. It surfaces in other ways.

And so, Scripture says, we find ourselves in a civil war of desire. The horrors of this war go well beyond spoiled dinners and a little marital tension. We will sacrifice anything on the altar of our anger, the rage that is slowly building from a lifetime of thwarted desire—our marriages, our child's self-esteem, someone's very life. At the same moment that Krakauer's com-panions were battling for their lives on Everest's southeast ridge, three Indian climbers were stranded by the storm on the other side of the mountain as they attempted the summit from the northeast. Unable to work their way down, they spent the night on the face of the mountain without shelter in a howling blizzard. The following morning, two Japanese climbers ascending by the same route came across the climbers, now near death. They offered no assistance; no food or water, no bottled oxygen. They didn't even speak to them, but stepped aside and took their rest a few hundred feet beyond. The Japanese climbers made the summit; then they left the Indians to die as they passed them again on their way back down.

There is a reason Jesus chose lust and murder as examples of what happens when desire goes mad within us. He knew what our desperate hearts naturally do when our desires come into conflict. He knew to what lengths we would go to seek satisfaction of our soul's hunger. For the battle of desire rages not only between us, but *within* us.

THE BEAST WITHIN

Jeremy called and asked to see me to talk about "a little financial problem" he was having. I told him, sure, I could spare an hour of my Saturday. I thought he might need a small loan or some help with his checkbook. But when I saw the look on his face, I knew an hour wasn't going to be enough. Jeremy's little problem was that he had taken every credit card he owned to the limit, accumulating thousands of dollars in debt. Knowing he was unemployed at the time, with no prospect at all of paying off such a load, he was panic-stricken. "Good grief," I asked, "how did it happen?" The story proved more outrageous than the debt. He had booked himself a week at a five-star resort. Posing as a wealthy physician, Jeremy entertained a variety of women—"gold diggers"—purchasing their affections with lavish gifts and gourmet dinners. By the end of his self-created fantasy island trip he had lost his integrity and about ten thousand dollars.

I would never have believed it unless he himself had told me, through tears of shame and regret. He is a quiet and unassuming man, the complete opposite of some jet-setting gigolo. No one would have dreamed he was capable of such a thing. But then again, we wonder: *What am I capable of? Dare I even begin to feel my desire?* We may not go so far, but we know that there is a ravenous beast within us. Years of living in an indifferent and often hostile world create a deep sense of unsettledness within us. A friend asked the other day: "How important are feelings of desire? I ask because I have a seeming overabundance of desire, but it sometimes goes astray in a crazed and hopeless pursuit of brownies or something of the sort."

> Something has gone wrong deep within me and gets the better of me every time. It happens so regularly that it's predictable. The moment I decide to do good, sin is there to trip me up. I truly delight in God's commands, but it's pretty obvious that not all of me joins in that delight. Parts of me covertly rebel, and just when I least expect it, they take charge. (Rom. 7:20–23 *The Message*)

> For the sinful nature desires what is contrary to the Spirit, and the Spirit what is contrary to the sinful nature. They are in conflict with each other, so that you do not do what you want. (Gal. 5:17 NIV)

There is a nagging awareness inside us, warning that we'd better not feel our hunger too deeply or it will undo us. We might do something crazed, desperate. We are caught on the horns of a dilemma; our unmet desires are a source of trouble, and it feels as if it will get worse if we allow ourselves to feel how much we do desire. Not only that, we often don't even know what we desire. Dan, a passionate young friend now finishing college, just sent this E-mail:

> Chris McCandless wrote, "All hail the Phantom Bear, the beast within us all." Well the "Bear" so to speak has really been growling loud as of late. I seem to be daily wanting more out of my life than what I have been living. Leo Tolstoy wrote, "I felt in myself a superabundance of energy which found no outlet in my

quiet life." And that really describes me well. I want more . . . more of God in my life . . . more intimacy with my friends . . . and I feel bad for wanting it. Everyone seems so content here and simple . . . and also I feel like I'm longing for nothing I'm certain of.

We try food, tennis, television, or sex, going from one thing to another, never quite finding satisfaction. The reason we don't know what we want is that we're so *unacquainted* with our desire. We try to keep a safe distance between our daily lives and our heart's desire because it causes us so much trouble. We're surprised by our anger and threatened by what feels like a ravenous bear within us. Do we really want to open Pandora's box? If you remember the Greek myth, Pandora was the wife of Epimetheus, given to him by Zeus. The gods provided many gifts to her, including a mysterious box, which she was warned never to open. Eventually, her curiosity got the better of her, and she lifted the lid. Immediately, a host of evils flew out, plagues against the mind and body of mankind. She tried to close the box, but to no avail; the troubles had been loosed.

Dare we awaken our hearts to their true desires? Dare we come alive? Is it better, as the saying goes, to have loved and lost than never to have loved at all? We're not so sure. After his divorce, a friend's father decided to remain single the rest of his life. He told his son, "It's easier to stay out than to get out." Our dilemma is this: we can't seem to live with desire, and we can't live without it. In the face of this quandary most people decide to bury the whole question and put as much distance as they can between themselves and their desires. It is a logical and tragic act. The tragedy is increased tenfold when this suicide of soul is committed under the conviction that this is precisely what Christianity recommends. We have never been more mistaken.

Had you journeyed in those days through the barren lands, you might have seen the sea lion for yourself. Quite often in the evening, he would go and sit upon his favorite rock, a very large boulder, which lifted him off the burning sand and allowed him a view of the entire country.

There he would remain for hours into the night, silhouetted against the sky. And on the best nights, when the wind shifted to the east, a faint smell of salt air would come to him on the breeze. Then he would close his eyes and imagine himself once more at the sea. When he lay himself down to sleep, he would dream of a vast, deep ocean. Twisting and turning, diving and twirling, he would swim and swim and swim. When he woke, he thought he heard the sound of breakers.

The sea was calling to him.

CHAPTER THREE

DARE WE DESIRE?

But for real proof you must look at your own longings and aspirations; you must listen to the deep themes of your own life story.

—Gerald May

Longing is the heart's treasury.

—Augustine

What do you want?

—Jesus of Nazareth

The shriveled figure lay in the sun like a pile of rags dumped there by accident. It hardly appeared to be human. But those who used the gate to go in and out of Jerusalem recognized him. It was his spot and had been for as long as anyone could remember. He was disabled, dropped off there every morning by someone in his family, and picked up again at the end of the day. Over the years, a sort of gallery of human brokenness gathered by the pool of Bethesda—the lame, the blind, the deaf, lepers, you name it. A rumor was going around that sometimes (no one really knew when) an angel would stir the waters, and the first one in would be healed. Sort of a lottery, if you will. And as with every lottery, the desperate gathered round, hoping for a miracle. So—technically speaking—the man was never alone. But it had been so long since anyone had actually *spoken* to him, he thought the question was meant for someone else. Squinting upward into the sun, he didn't recognize the figure standing above him. The misshapen man asked the fellow to repeat himself; perhaps he had misheard. Although the voice was kind, the question felt harsh, even cruel.

"Do you want to get well?"

He sat speechless, blinking into the sun. Slowly, the words seeped into his consciousness, like a voice calling him out of a dream. *Do I want to get well?* Slowly, like a wheel long rusted, his mind began to turn over. *What kind of question is that? Why else would I be lying here? Why else would I have spent every day for the past thirty-eight seasons lying here? He is mocking me.* The man was familiar with mockery and had endured his share of ridicule. But now that his vision had adjusted to the glare, he could see the inquisitor's face, his eyes. There was no hint of mockery. The face was as kind as the voice he heard. Apparently, the man meant what he said, and he was waiting for an answer. "Do you want to get well? What is it that you want?"

"Hey, there, you without the legs—what are you lying here for? Wouldn't you love to get up, stretch yourself a bit, have a walk around?" Who dared ask something so callous? It was Jesus who posed the question, so there must be something we're missing here. He is love incarnate. Why did he ask the paraplegic such an embarrassing question? Of course the fellow wanted to get well. You don't have to be God to see the obvious. Or was it? As with most of the questions he posed, Jesus was probing for something we do not see. He knew the answer, of course—but did the man? Do we? Think of the fellow on the ground for a moment; put yourself, literally, in his shoes. His entire life has been shaped by his brokenness. All his days he has wanted one thing. Forget riches. Forget fame. Life for this man was captured in one simple, unreachable desire. When the other children ran and played, he sat and watched. When his family stood at the temple to pray, he lay on the ground. Every time he needed to have a drink or to go to the bathroom, someone had to pick him up and take him there.

So he had gone there for the past thirty-eight years, hoping to hit the jackpot. Sure, it was a long shot, but it was all he had. At what point did he begin to lose hope? First a year, then two went by. Nothing, at least for him. Maybe someone else got a miracle; that would buy him some time. What about after five years with no results? Ten? How long can we sustain desire against continual disappointment? Some hold out longer than others, but eventually, we all move to a place of resignation or cynicism or bitterness. As the years rolled on, this man, like all of us, began to lose any vital heart-connection to what he wanted. He was present, but not accounted for. The calluses had formed—not in the heart of Jesus, but over the man's heart. He had abandoned desire. Jesus took him back into the secret of his own heart. By asking him what he wanted, Jesus took the man *back into* his desire. Why?

It is where we must go if we are to meet God.

AN INVITATION TO DESIRE

This may come as a surprise to you: Christianity is not an invitation to become a moral person. It is not a program for getting us in line or for reforming society. It has a powerful effect upon our lives, but when transformation comes, it is always the *aftereffect* of something else, something at the level of our hearts. At its core, Christianity begins with an invitation to *desire*. Look again at the way Jesus relates to people. As he did with the fellow at the Sheep Gate, he is continually taking them into their hearts, to their deepest desires.

The story of the two blind men on the road to Jericho repeats the theme. Jesus is passing by the spot where these two men have sat looking for a handout for who knows how long. They learn that Jesus is going by, and they cry out for him. Though the crowd tries to shut them up, they succeed in shouting over the ruckus and capturing the Master's attention. The parade stops. Jesus steps to the side of the road, and standing there before him are two men, nothing clearer than the fact that they are blind. "What do you want me to do for you?" Again the question. Again the obvious that must not be so obvious after all.

Then there is the Samaritan woman whom Jesus meets at the well. She has come alone in the heat of the day to draw water, and they both know why. By coming when the sun is high, she is less likely to run into anyone. You see, her sexual lifestyle has earned her a "reputation." Back in those days, having one partner after another wasn't looked so highly upon. She's on her sixth lover, and so she'd rather bear the scorching rays of the sun than face the searing words of the "decent" women of the town who come at evening to draw water. She succeeds in avoiding the women, but runs into God instead. What does he choose to talk to her about—her immorality? No, he speaks to her about her *thirst*: "If you knew the generosity of God and who I am, you would be asking *me* for a drink, and I would give you fresh, living water" (John 4:10 *The Message*). Remarkable. He doesn't give a little sermon about purity; he doesn't even mention it, except to say that he knows what her life has been like: "You've had five husbands, and the man you're living with now isn't even your husband" (John 4:18 *The Message*). In other words, now that we both know it, let's talk about your heart's real thirst, since the life you've chosen obviously isn't working. "The water I give will be an artesian spring within, gushing fountains of endless life" (John 4:14 *The Message*).

Later in the gospel of John, Jesus extends the offer to anyone who realizes that his life just isn't touching his deep desire: "If you are thirsty, come to me! If you believe in me, come and drink! For the Scriptures declare that rivers of living water will flow out from within" (John 7:37–38 NLT). His message wasn't something new, but it confounded the religious leaders of the day. Surely, those scripturally learned Jews must have recalled God's long-standing invitation to them, spoken seven hundred years earlier through the prophet Isaiah:

> Come, all you who are thirsty,
>> come to the waters;
> and you who have no money,
>> come, buy and eat!
> Come, buy wine and milk
>> without money and without cost.
> Why spend money on what is not bread,
>> and your labor on what does not satisfy?
> Listen, listen to me, and eat what is good,
>> and your soul will delight in the richest of fare.
>> (Isa. 55:1–2 NIV)

Somehow, the message had gotten lost by the time Jesus showed up on the scene. The Jews of his day were practicing a very soul-killing spirituality, a lifeless religion of duty and obligation. They had abandoned desire and replaced it with knowledge and performance as the key to life. The synagogue was the place to go to learn how to get with the program. Desire was out of the question; duty was the path that people must walk. No wonder they feared Jesus. He came along and started *appealing* to desire.

To the weary, Jesus speaks of rest. To the lost, he speaks of finding your way. Again and again and again, Jesus takes people back to their desires: "Ask and it will be given to you; seek and you will find; knock and the door will be opened to you" (Matt. 7:7 NIV). These are outrageous words, provocative words. *Ask, seek, knock*—these words invite and *arouse* desire. What is it that you *want*? They fall on deaf ears if there is nothing you want, nothing you're looking for, nothing you're hungry enough to bang on a door over.

Jesus provokes desire; he awakens it; he heightens it. The religious watchdogs accuse him of heresy. He says, "Not at all. This *is* the invitation God has been sending all along." He continues,

> You have your heads in your Bibles constantly because you think you'll find eternal life there. But you miss the forest for the trees. These Scriptures are all about *me*! And here I am, standing right before you, and you aren't willing to receive from me the life you say you want. (John 5:39–40 *The Message*)

LIFE IN ALL ITS FULLNESS

Eternal life—we tend to think of it in terms of existence that never comes to an end. And the existence it seems to imply—a sort of religious experience in the sky—leaves us wondering if we *would* want it to go on forever. But Jesus is quite clear that when he speaks of eternal life, what he means is life that is absolutely wonderful and can never be diminished or stolen from you. He says, "I have come that they may have life, and have it to the full" (John 10:10 NIV). Not, "I have come to threaten you into line," or "I have come to exhaust you with a long list of demands." Not even, "I have come primarily to forgive you." But simply, *My purpose is to bring you life in all its fullness.* Dallas Willard writes in *The Divine Conspiracy*,

Jesus offers himself as God's doorway into the life that is truly life. Confidence in him leads us today, as in other times, to become his apprentices in eternal living. "Those who come through me will be safe," he said. "They will go in and out and find all they need. I have come into their world that they may have life, and life to the limit."

In other words, eternal life is not primarily *duration* but *quality* of life, "life to the limit." It cannot be stolen from us, and so it does go on. But the focus is on the life itself. "In him was life," the apostle John said of Jesus, "and that life was the light of men" (John 1:4 NIV). Notice that the people who aren't so good at keeping up with the program but who are very aware of their souls' deep thirst are captured by Jesus' message. Common folk tear the roofs off houses to get to him. They literally trample each other in an effort to get closer to this man. I've never seen anyone acting like this in order to get a chance to serve on some church committee or to hear a sermon on why dancing is "of the devil." People act like this when it's a matter of life and death. Crowds trample each other to get out of a burning building; they press into the mob to reach a food line. When life is at stake and the answer is within reach, that's when you see human desire unmasked in all its desperation.

The Pharisees miss the boat entirely. Their hearts are hardened by the very law they claimed would bring them life. They put their hope in rules and regulations, in knowing and doing things perfectly. Having killed their souls' thirst with duty, they went on to kill their souls' only Hope, thinking they were doing their duty.

GOOD NEWS THAT'S NOT REALLY

Things appear to have come full circle. The promise of life and the invitation to desire have again been lost beneath a pile of religious teachings that put the focus on knowledge and performance.

> History has brought us to the point where the Christian message is thought to be essentially concerned only with how to deal with sin: with wrongdoing or wrong-being and its effects. Life, our actual existence, is not included in what is now presented as the heart of the Christian message, or it is included only marginally. (*The Divine Conspiracy*)

Thus Willard describes the Gospels we have today as "gospels of sin management." Sin is the bottom line, and we have the cure. Typically, it is a system of knowledge or performance, or a mixture of both. Those in the knowledge camp put the emphasis on getting our doctrine in line. Right belief is seen as the means to life. Desire is irrelevant; *content* is what matters. But notice this—the Pharisees knew more about the Bible than most of us ever will, and it *hardened* their hearts. Knowledge just isn't all it's cracked up to be. If you are familiar with the biblical narrative, you will remember that there were two special trees in Eden—the Tree of Knowledge of Good and Evil and the Tree of Life. We got the wrong tree. We got knowledge, and it hasn't done us much good. T. S. Eliot lamented,

> Endless invention, endless experiment,
> Brings knowledge of motion, but not of stillness;
> Knowledge of speech, but not of silence;

Knowledge of words, and ignorance of the Word.
Where is the Life we have lost in living?
Where is the wisdom we have lost in knowledge?
                    ("Choruses from the Rock")

Christianity is often presented as essentially the transfer of a body of knowledge. We learn about where the Philistines were from, and how much a drachma would be worth today, and all sorts of things about the original Greek. The information presented could not seem more irrelevant to our deepest desires.

Then there are the systems aimed at getting our behavior in line, one way or another. Regardless of where you go to church, there is nearly always an unspoken list of what you shouldn't do (tailored to your denomination and culture, but typically rather long) and a list of what you may do (usually much shorter—mostly religious activity that seems totally unrelated to our deepest desires and leaves us only exhausted).

And this, we are told, is the good news. Know the right thing; do the right thing. This is life? When it doesn't strike us as something to get excited about, we feel we must not be spiritual enough. Perhaps once we have kept the list long enough, we will understand.

We don't need more facts, and we certainly don't need more things to do. We need *Life*, and we've been looking for it ever since we lost Paradise. Jesus appeals to our desire because he came to speak to it. When we abandon desire, we no longer hear or understand what he is saying. But we have returned to the message of the synagogue; we are preaching the law. And desire is the enemy. After all, desire is the single major hindrance to the goal—getting us in line. We are told to kill desire and call it sanctification. Or as Jesus put it to the Pharisees, "You load people down with rules and regulations, nearly breaking their backs,

41

but never lift even a finger to help" (Luke 11:46 *The Message*). As a result, Willard says, "The souls of human beings are left to shrivel and die on the plains of life because they are not introduced into the environment for which they were made."

"I began to seriously question my faith," wrote a friend, "when I was suffering my second year of depression. People in church saw my depressed face, and they complimented me on how I was such a good Christian." I am not making this up. This poor fellow was actually cheered for doing well spiritually when it became apparent his soul was dying. "I thought the best way for a person to live is to keep his desires to a minimum so that he will be prepared to serve God." Isn't that the message? It may not be explicit (what we truly believe rarely is), but it's clear enough. Get rid of desire, and get with the program.

Compare the shriveled life held up as a model of Christian maturity with the life revealed in the book of Psalms:

> You have made known to me the path of life;
> you will fill me with joy in your presence,
> with eternal pleasures at your right hand.
>
> (16:11 NIV)

> As the deer pants for streams of water,
> so my soul pants for you, O God.
> My soul thirsts for God, for the living God.
> When can I go and meet with God?
>
> (42:1–2 NIV)

> O God, you are my God,
> earnestly I seek you;
> My soul thirsts for you,
> my body longs for you,

in a dry and weary land,
where there is no water.
(63:1 NIV)

Ask yourself, Could this person be promoted to a position of leadership in my church? Heavens, no. He is far too unstable, too passionate, too desirous. It's all about pleasure and desire and thirst. And David, who wrote most of the psalms, was called by God a "man after his own heart" (1 Sam. 13:14 NIV).

Christianity has nothing to say to the person who is completely happy with the way things are. Its message is for those who hunger and thirst—for those who desire life as it was meant to be. Why does Jesus appeal to desire? Because it is essential to his goal: bringing us life. He heals the fellow at the pool of Bethesda, by the way. The two blind men get their sight, and the woman at the well finds the love she has been seeking. Reflecting on these events, the apostle John looked at what Jesus offered and what he delivered and said, "He who has the Son has life" (1 John 5:12 NIV).

THE STORY OF DESIRE

We misunderstand the good news Jesus announced when we hear it outside the story God is telling. Good news, a report that brings us relief and joy at the same time, is news that speaks to our dilemma. Hearing from your doctor that the lump is benign is good news. Receiving a notice from the IRS that you will not be audited after all is good news. Getting a call from the police to say that they've found your daughter is good news. Being offered tips and techniques for living a more dutiful life isn't even in the field of good news. We know in our hearts that our dilemma cannot be, "I sure wish I could be a more decent chap.

What I really need is a program to improve my morals." Now, Jesus seemed to think that what he was offering really and truly spoke to our dilemma. Those who grasped what he was saying agreed. So what is our dilemma? What do we need most desperately to hear? Where are we in the story?

Let us ask the storytellers. In many ways, Hollywood has mastered the art of speaking to the human predicament. Consider the success of James Cameron's 1997 film *Titanic*. Not only did it sweep the Oscars, but the movie has become the all-time leading box office hit, passing even *Gone with the Wind*. Ticket sales have reached nearly $2 billion. I know people who have seen it not once or twice, but multiple times. It is a phenomenon whose appeal surpassed generational and cultural boundaries. Why? Christian critiques of the film missed the mark entirely, focusing almost exclusively on moral issues (sin management brought to film review). I cannot help thinking that if those reviewers were at the well when the Samaritan woman came by, they would have given her an earful.

But much more is going on here. Obviously, the film touched a nerve; it tapped into the reservoir of human longing for life. What is its story line? The film begins with romance, a story of passionate love, set within an exciting journey. Those who saw *Titanic* will recall the scene early in the film where the two lovers are standing on the prow of the great ship as it slices through a golden sea into a luscious sunset. Romance, beauty, adventure. Eden. The life we've all been searching for because it's the life we all were made for. Have we forgotten—or never been told? Once upon a time, in the beginning of humanity's sojourn on earth, we lived in a garden that was exotic and lush, inviting and full of adventure. It was "the environment for which we were made," as the sea lion was made for the sea. Now, those of you who learned about Eden in Sunday school maybe missed something here. Using flannel graphs to depict Paradise somehow doesn't do it. Picture Maui at sunset with your dearest love. A world of intimacy and beauty and adventure.

But then tragedy strikes. I'm sure I won't ruin the story for anyone if I tell you the ship goes down. How awful, how haunting are those scenes of the slow but irreversible plunge of the great ocean liner, leaving behind a sea of humanity to freeze to death in the Arctic waters. Everything is gone—the beauty, the romance, the adventure. Paradise is lost. And we know it. More than ever before, we know it. There was a time earlier in this century when we believed in the future, in something called progress. Not anymore, especially not the younger generations. I have yet to meet a young person who believes that his life will be better in a few years. As Chesterton said, we all somehow know that we are the "survivors of a wreck, the crew of a golden ship that had gone down before the beginning of the world." The ship has gone down. We are all adrift in the water, hoping to find some wreckage to crawl upon to save ourselves.

But that is not all. The secret of the film's success is found in the final scene. As the camera takes us once more to the bottom of the sea and we are given a last look at the rotting hulk of the once great ship, something happens. The *Titanic* begins to transform before our eyes. Light floods in through the windows. The rust and decay melt away as the pristine beauty of the ship is restored. The doors fly open, and there are all the great hearts of the story, not dead at all, but quite alive and rejoicing. A party is under way; a wedding party. The heroine, dressed in a beautiful white gown, ascends the staircase into the embrace of her lover. Everything is restored. Tragedy does not have the final word. Somehow, beyond all hope, Paradise has been regained.

Isn't this our dilemma? Isn't this the news we have been longing for? A return of the life we prize? Look again at what Jesus offers. There is bread enough for everyone. There is healing for every brokenness. The lost are found. The weary are given rest. There is life available—life to the limit.

> I am the Gate. Anyone who goes through me will be cared for—will freely go in and out, and find pasture. A thief is only there to steal and kill and destroy. I came so they can have real and eternal life, more and better life than they ever dreamed of. (John 10:9–10 *The Message*)

DESIRE AND GOODNESS

But doesn't Christianity condemn desire—the Puritans and all that? Not at all. Quite the contrary. Christianity takes desire seriously, far more seriously than the Stoic or the mere hedonist. Christianity refuses to budge from the fact that man was made for pleasure, that his beginning and his end is a paradise, and that the goal of living is to find Life. Jesus knows the dilemma of desire, and he speaks to it in nearly everything he says.

When it comes to the moral question, it is not simply whether we say yes or no to desire, but always what we *do* with desire. Christianity recognizes that we have desire gone mad within us. But it does not seek to rectify the problem by killing desire; rather, it seeks the healing of desire, just as it seeks the healing of every other part of our human being.

"Two things contribute to our sanctification," wrote Pascal. "Pains and pleasures." And while we know that our journey is strewn with danger and difficulty, "the difficulties they meet with are not without pleasure, *and cannot be overcome without pleasure*." Where do you find Jesus saying, "The problem with you people is, you want too much. If you'd just learn to be happy with less, we'd all get along just fine"? Not anywhere. Quite the contrary. "My commands are for your good," he says, "always."

Something has gone wrong in us, very wrong indeed. So wrong that we have to be told that joy is found not in having another man's wife, but in having our own. But the point is not the law; the point is the joy. Need I say more than this: modern Christianity has brought an entire group of people to the point where they have to be told that sex is, in the words of one book, "intended for pleasure."

God is realistic. He knows that ecstasy is not an option; we are made for bliss, and we must have it, one way or another. He also knows that happiness is fragile and rests upon a foundation greater than happiness. All the Christian disciplines were formulated at one time or another in an attempt to heal desire's waywardness and so, by means of obedience, bring us home to bliss. Walter Brueggemann suggests that faith on its way to maturity moves from "duty to delight." If it is not moving, then it has become stagnant. If it has changed the goal from delight to duty, it has gone backward; it is *regressing*. This is the great lost truth of the Christian faith, that correction of Judaism made by Jesus and passed on to us: the goal of morality is not morality—it is ecstasy. *You* are intended for pleasure!

WHO, THEN, CAN BE SAVED?

Look again at the story Jesus told about the prodigal son. It might be called the story of desire. Consider what each character does with his desire. You have the younger son, whose desires get him into a world of trouble. Then there is the father, whose desire for the lost boy is so deep that he sees him coming from a long way off—he has been watching, waiting. Forgiveness is assumed; it's a given. He's grateful just to have the boy home again. And then there is the older brother. He's the party pooper, if you recall. His younger brother is "back from the dead," as the

father says, and the older brother won't even come in for the cel-
ebration. He stands outside, sulking. Let's pick up the story there:

> The older brother was angry and wouldn't go in. His father came
> out and begged him, but he replied, "All these years I've worked
> hard for you and never once refused to do a single thing you told
> me to. And in all that time you never gave me even one young
> goat for a feast with my friends. Yet when this son of yours
> comes back after squandering your money on prostitutes, you
> celebrate by killing the finest calf we have." His father said to
> him, "Look, dear son, you and I are very close, and everything I
> have is yours. We had to celebrate this happy day. For your
> brother was dead and has come back to life! He was lost, but
> now he is found!" (Luke 15:28–32 NLT)

The older brother is the picture of the man who has lived his
entire life from duty and obligation. When the wayward son
returns from his shipwreck of desire, his brother is furious
because he gets a party and not a trip behind the barn with the
broadside of a paddle. He tells his father that he has been had;
that all these years he hasn't gotten a thing in return for his life
of service. The father's reply cuts to the chase: "All that is mine
has always been yours." In other words, "You never asked."
Rembrandt captures all this powerfully in his now-famous painting *The Return of the Prodigal Son*. In the painting, the elder brother
stands a step *above* the reunion of father and son. He will not step
down, enter in. He is above it all. But who receives redemption?
The scandalous message of the story is this: those who kill
desire—the legalists, the dutiful—are not the ones who experience the father's embrace. The question is not, Dare we desire,
but dare we *not* desire?

The sea lion loved his rock, and he even loved waiting night after night for the sea breezes that might come. Especially he loved the dreams those memories would stir. But as you well know, even the best of dreams cannot go on, and in the morning when the sea lion woke, he was still in the barren lands. Sometimes he would close his eyes and try to fall back asleep. It never seemed to work, for the sun was always very bright.

Eventually, it became too much for him to bear. He began to visit his rock only on occasion. "I have too much to do," he told himself. "I cannot waste my time just idling about." He really did not have so much to do. The truth of it was, waking so far from home was such a disappointment, he did not want to have those wonderful dreams anymore. The day finally came when he stopped going to his rock altogether, and he no longer lifted his nose to the wind when the sea breezes blew.

CHAPTER FOUR

DISOWNED DESIRE

The danger is that the soul should persuade itself that it is not hungry. It can only persuade itself of this by lying.
—*Simone Weil*

Everybody's got a hungry heart.
—*Bruce Springsteen*

In his essay "Screwtape Proposes a Toast," C. S. Lewis portrays the old devil delivering the annual commencement speech for the Tempter's Training College for Young Devils. Screwtape begins his address by lamenting that "the human souls on whose anguish we have been feasting tonight were of a pretty poor quality." He laments that there are so few truly great sinners available at present; they could capture only passive milksops.

> Here were vermin so muddled in mind, so passively responsive to environment, that it was very hard to raise them to that level of clarity and deliberateness at which mortal sin becomes possible. To raise them just enough; but not that fatal millimeter of "too much." For then of course all might possibly have been lost. They might have seen; they might have repented.

Screwtape decides that perhaps this is all for the best because there are real dangers when a soul is capable of deep desire. He

knows what we have forgotten: "The great (and toothsome) sinners are made out of the very same material as those horrible
phenomena, the great Saints."

Dare we forget King David? Yes, his passions got him in a heap
of trouble—and gave us our book of *worship*, the Psalms. Sure, Peter
was a hotheaded disciple always quick with a reply. Remember in
the Garden of Gethsemane—he's the one who lopped off the ear
of the high priest's servant. But he was also the first to acknowledge
that Jesus was the Messiah, and despite his Good Friday betrayals,
he became a key apostle, contributed important pieces to the
Scripture, and followed Jesus all the way to his own crucifixion,
asking to be nailed to the cross upside down because he was not
worthy to die in the manner of his Lord. Surely, we remember that
Paul was once Saul, the fiery young Pharisee "advancing in Judaism
beyond many Jews of my own age and . . . extremely zealous for
the traditions of my fathers" (Gal. 1:14 NIV). His zeal made him the
foremost persecutor of the church. When Christ knocked him off
his donkey on the Damascus road, Paul was hunting down the
church, "uttering threats with every breath" (Acts 9:1 NLT). Christ
captured his zeal, and after Damascus it led him to work "harder
than all the other apostles" (1 Cor. 15:10 NLT).

Augustine was also a passionate young man, sexually licen-
tious, enamored with the pleasures of Rome, "scratching the sore
of lust," as he would call it after Christ got hold of him. He went
on to become one of the great pillars of the church, laying the
foundation for the rise of Christendom after the fall of Rome.
"Tempered in the fires of his own sensuality, toughened by his
arduous explorations of the heresies of the age," he became,
in Malcolm Muggeridge's words, "a latter-day Noah . . . constrained to construct an ark, in his case Orthodoxy, wherein
the Church could survive through the dark days that lay ahead"
(*A Third Testament*).

The great saints come from the same material as the "tooth-some sinners." Desire, a burning passion for more, is at the heart of both. Those who would kill the passion altogether would murder the very essence that makes heroes of the faith. They remind me of those misguided physicians of a hundred years ago, who would attempt to cure a fever by "bleeding" their patients, cutting a vein and draining them of bowls of blood, depriving them of the very life force they needed to get better. It's a wonder so many survived. Augustine would later write,

> Give me a man in love; he knows what I mean. Give me one who yearns; give me one who is hungry; give me one far away in this desert, who is thirsty and sighs for the spring of the Eternal Country. Give me that sort of man; he knows what I mean. But if I speak to a cold man, he just doesn't know what I am talking about. (Quoted by Muggeridge in *A Third Testament*)

BLESSED ARE THE NICE?

And so Screwtape reveals the enemy's ploy—first make humans flabby, with small passions and desires, then offer a sop to those diminished passions so that their experience is one of contentment. They know nothing of great joy or great sorrow. They are merely *nice*. One young woman wrote to me,

> My parents always told me to be a "nice little girl." I simply assumed that being nice meant not getting upset or being angry with anyone . . . I was nice because I wanted to be liked, and I figured that people would like someone who was always nice. My senior year of high school I was voted "Nicest Senior" for the senior awards, and it was true. I was nice and I was proud of it. I thought there was no higher virtue than niceness.

Christianity has come to the point where we believe that there is no higher aspiration for the human soul than to be nice. We are producing a generation of men and women whose greatest virtue is that they don't offend anyone. Then we wonder why there is not more passion for Christ. How can we hunger and thirst after righteousness if we have ceased hungering and thirsting altogether? As C. S. Lewis said, "We castrate the gelding and bid him be fruitful."

The greatest enemy of holiness is not passion; it is apathy. Look at Jesus. He was no milksop. His life was charged with passion. After he drove the crooks from the temple, "his disciples remembered that it is written: 'Zeal for your house will consume me'" (John 2:17 NIV). This isn't quite the pictures we have in Sunday school, Jesus with a lamb and a child or two, looking for all the world like Mr. Rogers with a beard. The world's nicest guy. He was something far more powerful. He was holy. G. K. Chesterton wrote,

> Instead of looking at books and pictures about the New Testament I looked at the New Testament. There I found an account, not in the least of a person with His hair parted in the middle or His hands clasped in appeal, but of an extraordinary being with lips of thunder and acts of lurid decision, flinging down tables, casting out devils, passing with the wild scenery of the wind from mountain isolation to a sort of dreadful demagogy; a being who acted like an angry god—and always like a god . . . The diction used about Christ has been . . . sweet and submissive. But the diction used by Christ is quite gigantesque; it is full of camels leaping through needles and mountains hurled into the sea. (*Orthodoxy*)

If the way to avoid the murderous rage and deceptive allures of desire is to kill it, if deadness is next to godliness, then Jesus had to be the deadest person ever. But he is called the *living* God. "It is a dreadful thing," the writer of Hebrews says, "to fall into the hands of the living God . . . For our 'God is a consuming fire'" (Heb. 10:31; 12:29 NIV). And what is this consuming fire? His jealous love (Deut. 4:24). God is a deeply, profoundly passionate person. Zeal consumes him. It is the secret of his life, the writer of Hebrews says. The "joy set before him" enabled Jesus to endure the agony of the Cross (Heb. 12:2 NIV). In other words, his profound desire for something greater sustained him at the moment of his deepest trial. We cannot hope to live like him without a similar depth of passion. Many people find that the dilemma of desire is too much to live with, and so they abandon, they disown their desire. This is certainly true of a majority of Christians at present. Somehow we believe that we can get on without it. We are mistaken.

THE MAN WHO WANTED NOTHING

Initially, Gary and Jill had come to me because their marriage had become merely functional. No major issues—no one was throwing dishes; neither was having an affair. As I realized later, that would have been better, at least a sign of life. Their marriage had all the passion of yesterday's oatmeal. Jill was the one who called because she was afraid that she was losing Gary, that they were "drifting apart." It didn't take long to see why. Gary had checked out. He was still going to work, paying the bills, and cutting the grass, but that was it. There was no emotion, no investment, no reaction to anything. The more vital parts of him were shut down. I asked if he and I might spend some time just talking about his life. As the weeks rolled by, I learned that he had been a faithful church attender, never missing a Sunday. He served on a committee and offered help to those in need. But obviously, something was missing.

I was surprised, frankly, when he showed up each week. Going to counseling can feel like the emotional equivalent of attempting Everest, but I found in him nothing near the desire to make the ascent. After months of getting nowhere, I asked the obvious: "Gary, why are you a Christian?" He sat in silence for what must have been five minutes. "I don't know. I guess because it's the right thing to do." "Is there anything you're hoping to enjoy as a result of your faith?" "No . . . not really." "So what is it that you *want*, Gary?" An even longer silence. I waited patiently. "I don't desire anything." Our sessions ended shortly thereafter, and I felt bad that I was unable to help him. You cannot help someone who doesn't want a thing. All his life Gary had been a good boy. A gelding. And geldings, though they are nicer and much more well behaved than stallions, do not bring life. They are sterile.

I thought of the last story we have from the life of the prophet Elisha. Jehoash was king of Israel at the time, and he went to visit Elisha on his sickbed. He knew that without the help of the great prophet, the future of Israel was looking dim. Enemies were closing in on every side, waiting for the kill. Elisha told the king to take in hand some arrows.

> And the king took them. Elisha told him, "Strike the ground." He struck it three times and stopped. The man of God was angry with him and said, "You should have struck the ground five or six times; then you would have defeated [your enemies] completely . . . But now you will defeat [them] only three times." Elisha died and was buried. (2 Kings 13:18–20 NIV)

That's it? What a strange story! Why was the old prophet so angry? Because the king was nonchalant; he was passionless, indifferent. He gave the ground a whack or two. His heart wasn't in it. God says, in effect, "If that is how little you care about the future of your people, that is all the help you will get." In other words, if your heart's not in it, well then, neither is mine. You can't lead a country, let alone flourish in a marriage, with an attitude like that. To abandon desire is to say, "I don't really need you; I don't really want you. But I will live with you because, well, I'm supposed to." It is a grotesque corruption of what was meant to be a beautiful dance between desire and devotion.

Your heart longs, and you go to seek the one you desire. She responds to your seeking because it touches her heart's desire to be longed for. Yes, commitment plays a vital role—but only as the *expression* of desire. Duty reduces the dance to a drill. It's as if you showed up with a bouquet of flowers for your anniversary. Your wife is delighted, but then you say, "Think nothing of it, my dear. It's my obligation." John Piper opens his book *Desiring God* with this illustration, showing the deadly effect of duty on a relationship: "Dutiful roses are a contradiction in terms." A woman doesn't want to be an object of duty; she wants to be *desired*. So does God. Thus A. W. Tozer asserted, "God waits to be wanted."

At one point I had asked Gary about his prayer life. "I never ask God for anything," he replied. I wasn't surprised. You see, the real dilemma of desire is that it *humbles* us. It takes us way beyond our own resources where we need to ask for help.

FAITH AS DESIRE

You may recall the story Jesus told of the man who entrusted three of his servants with thousands of dollars (literally, "talents"), urging them to handle his affairs well while he was away. When he returned, he listened eagerly to their reports. The first two fellows went out into the marketplace and doubled their investment. As a result, they were handsomely rewarded.

The third servant was not so fortunate. His gold was taken from him, and he was thrown into "outer darkness, where there will be weeping and gnashing of teeth." My goodness. Why? All he did was bury the money under the porch until his master's return. Most of us would probably agree with the path he chose—at least the money was safe there. But listen to his reasoning. Speaking to his master, he said, "I know you are a hard man, harvesting crops you didn't plant and gathering crops you didn't cultivate. I was afraid I would lose your money, so I hid it." (See Matt. 25:14–30 NLT.) He was afraid of the master, whom he saw as a hard man. He didn't trust his master's heart.

The issue isn't capital gains—it's what we think of God. When we bury our desires, we are saying the same thing: "God, I don't dare desire because I fear you; I think you are hard-hearted."

Just yesterday evening I was taking a walk in our neighborhood, talking to the Lord about going forward and establishing the ranch I have mentioned. I had been moving toward the creation of this place of ministry in what felt like sheer obedience, dragging my heart along behind me. God had been confirming the direction with many signs and affirmations. And yet I sensed that something was wrong. I was asking him what he wanted the ranch to be. He said, *What do you want it to be? What's in your heart?* I was embarrassed by the honesty of my reply: "What do you care about my desires?" There is this hurt and angry place inside, a very old wound, that harbors some rather strong doubts about how much God really cares for me.

We all have this place. Life has not turned out the way we want, and we know God could have handled things differently. Even though we may profess at one level a genuine faith in him, at another level we are like the third servant. Our obedience is not so much out of love as it is out of carefulness. "Just tell me what to do, God, and I'll do it." Killing desire may look like sanctification, but it's really godlessness. Literally, our way of handling life without God.

"But when the Son of Man comes, will he find faith on the earth?" Jesus had been talking about prayer by telling the story of a persistent widow who wasn't getting the justice she deserved from a belligerent judge. The woman won her case because she refused to let up. Jesus used her as a picture of unrelenting desire; he urged us not only to ask, but also to keep on asking. And then he ended the parable by wondering out loud, "When I return, will I find anyone who really lives by faith?" (see Luke 18:1–8 NIV).

We know in our hearts the connection he is making, though we haven't admitted it to ourselves. To live with desire is to choose vulnerability over self-protection; to admit our desire and seek help beyond ourselves is even more vulnerable. It is an act of trust. In other words, those who know their desire and refuse to kill it, or refuse to act as though they don't need help, they are the ones who live by faith. Those who do not ask do not trust God enough to desire. *They have no faith.* The deepest moral issue is always what we, in the heart of hearts, believe about God. And nothing reveals this belief as clearly as what we do with our desire.

PRAYER AS THE LANGUAGE OF DESIRE

The book of Hebrews describes the prayer life of Jesus in the following way: "While Jesus was here on earth, he offered prayers and pleadings, with a loud cry and tears, to the one who could deliver him" (5:7 NLT). That doesn't sound like the way that prayers are offered up in most churches on a typical Sunday morning. "Dear Lord, we thank you for this day, and we ask you to be with us in all we say and do. Amen." No pleading here, no loud cries and tears. Our prayers are cordial, modest, even reverent. Eugene Peterson calls them "cut-flower prayers." They are not like Jesus' prayers or, for that matter, like the psalms. The ranting and raving, the passion and ecstasy, the fury and desolation found in the psalms are so far from our religious expression that it seems hard to believe they were given to us as our *guide* to prayer. They seem so, well, *desperate*. Yet E. M. Bounds reminds us,

> Desire gives fervor to prayer. The soul cannot be listless when some great desire fixes and inflames it . . . Strong desires make strong prayers . . . The neglect of prayer is the fearful token of dead spiritual desires . . . There can be no true praying without desire. (*E. M. Bounds: Man of Prayer*)

A young woman came to see me, as most seeking counseling do, because she was at the end of her rope. What had begun a year earlier as mild depression had sunk deeper and deeper until she found herself contemplating suicide. We met for many weeks, and I came to know a delightful woman with a poet's heart, whose soul was buried beneath years not so much of tragedy but of neglect. This one particular afternoon, we had spoken for more than an hour of how deeply she longed for love, how almost completely ignored and misunderstood she felt her entire life. It was a tender, honest, and deeply moving session. As our time drew to a close, I asked her if she would pray with me. I could hardly believe what came next. She assumed a rather bland, religious tone to her voice and said something to the effect of "God, thank you for being here. Show me what I ought to do." I found myself speechless. *You've got to be kidding me,* I thought. *That's not how you feel at all. I know your heart's true cry. You are far more desperate than that.*

I wish she'd prayed like my son Luke. He is our youngest son and very wise for all of his five years. He knows what he wants and what it means to lose it. "My life is over." Luke laid his head down on the table and sighed, a picture of lament. I had just told him he couldn't have chocolate-covered sugar bombs for breakfast, and he was devastated. There was no longer any reason to go on. Life as he knew it was over. I enjoy Luke because he has more undisguised and unadulterated desire than anyone I know. He is "out there" with his desire and his disappointments. When we go over to someone's house for dinner, the first thing he'll ask will always be, "Is there dessert?" Part of me has tried to train this out of him; part of me admires the fact that he isn't embarrassed by his desire, like the rest of us. He is unashamed. We hide our true desire and call it maturity. Jesus is not impressed. He points to the less sophisticated attitude of a child as a better way to live.

Why are we so embarrassed by our desire? Why do we pretend that we're doing fine, thank you, that we don't need a thing? The persistent widow wasn't too proud to seek help. Neither was the psalmist. Their humility allowed them to express their desire. How little we come to God with what really matters to us. How rare it is that we even admit it to ourselves. "Is there dessert?" We don't pray like Jesus because we don't allow ourselves to be nearly so *alive*. We don't allow ourselves to feel how desperate our situation truly is. We sense that our desire will undo us if we let it rise up in all its fullness. Wouldn't it be better to bury the disappointment and the yearning and just get on with life? As Larry Crabb has pointed out, pretending seems a much more reliable road to Christian maturity. The only price we pay is a loss of soul, of communion with God, a loss of direction, and a loss of hope.

DRIFTING WITHOUT DESIRE

As a teacher, counselor, and author, I love what I do for a living. But it hasn't always been so. I spent a lifetime in Washington, D.C., several years ago. They were two of the most miserable years of my life. I don't like government, and I abhor politics. Harry Truman was right: "If you want a friend in Washington, buy a dog." What in the world was I doing there? I didn't really want to go; my employer talked me into accepting a transfer. But I can't put the blame on them. The truth is, I had come to a point where I didn't really know what I wanted in life. My real passion had been the theater, and for a number of years I pursued that dream with great joy. I had my own theater company and loved it. Through a series of events and what felt like betrayals, I had gotten deeply hurt. I left the theater and just went off to find a job. The Washington offer came up, and even though my heart wasn't in it, I let the opinions of people I admired dictate my course. Without a deep and burning desire of our own, we will be ruled by the desires of others.

Ann didn't know whether she should marry the man she was dating. They'd been dating for the last three years of college, and in many ways they enjoyed being together. But now that the possibility of engagement was becoming a reality, she found herself lost as to what she should do. "Do you want to marry him?" I asked. "I don't know. I guess so. I'm not sure." Ann is a very bright and energetic young woman. A youth pastor, she is rarely at a loss for ideas and energy. People regularly turn to her for counsel and encouragement. Ann always knows the "right" thing to do. But she was stumped. There was no "right" course to take. Her boyfriend was a committed Christian and a good man who loved her. She loved him too.

The problem was simply this: Ann had lived her entire life

based on what was right and had never once made a decision based on her desire. The oldest daughter in a family with some very high needs, Ann had been required to grow up much sooner than the others. She was highly responsible, and found her security in meeting the expectations and demands placed upon her. When the moment came for her to live out of her desire, she was out of practice. There was no one to tell her what to do.

I have met many Christians in the same position. I think of Charles, an attorney in his fifties who still doesn't know what he wants to be when he grows up. His wife left him last year. There is Paul, a young man in his twenties who doesn't know what to do with himself now that college is over. He focused on grades and left his heart behind. Jamie isn't sure if she should get married or stay single. Barbara hates her job but hasn't the slightest idea what she'd do if she left. They have all tried to bury their heart under the porch and seek a safer life. The poet David Whyte states,

> The hope is to stay in the background away from the fire, and wait for someone or something to come along and grant us immunity from these difficulties and sacrifices, someone to offer reassurance, saying perhaps, "Take the safe way, not the way of passion and creativity, as the path to your destiny, the life you desire. Follow it and you will never be touched . . ." [But] we cannot neglect our inner fire without damaging ourselves in the process. (*The Heart Aroused*)

The damage, of course, is a life lost unto itself. Millions of souls drifting through life, without an inner compass to give them direction. They take their cues from others and live out scripts from someone else's life. It's a high price to pay. Too high.

HOPELESS WITHOUT DESIRE

A curious warning is given to us in Peter's first epistle. There he tells us to be ready to give the reason for the hope that lies within us to everyone who asks (3:15). Now, what's strange about that passage is this: no one ever asks. When was the last time someone stopped you to inquire about the reason for the hope that lies within you? You're at the market, say, in the frozen food section. A friend you haven't seen for some time comes up to you, grasps you by both shoulders, and pleads, "Please, you've got to tell me. Be honest now. How can you live with such hope? Where does it come from? I must know the reason." In talking with hundreds of Christians, I've met only one or two who have experienced something like this.

Yet God tells us to be ready, so what's wrong? To be blunt, nothing about our lives is worth asking about. There's nothing intriguing about our hopes, nothing to make anyone curious. Not that we don't have hopes; we do. We hope we'll have enough after taxes this year to take a summer vacation. We hope our kids don't wreck the car. We hope our favorite team goes to the World Series. We hope our health doesn't give out, and so on. Nothing wrong with any of those hopes; nothing unusual, either. Everyone has hopes like that, so why bother asking us? It's life as usual. Sanctified resignation has become the new abiding place of contemporary Christians. No wonder nobody asks. Do *you* want the life of any Christian you know?

Having abandoned desire, we have lost hope. C. S. Lewis summed it up: "We can only hope for what we desire." No desire, no hope. Now, desire doesn't always translate into hope. There are many things I desire that I have little hope for. I desire to have lots more money than I do, but I see little reason to think it will come. But there isn't one thing I hope for that I don't *also* desire. This is Lewis's point. Bland assurances of the sweet by-and-by don't inflame the soul. Our hopes are deeply tied to our real desires, and so killing desire has meant a hopeless life for too many. It's as if we've already entered Dante's *Inferno*, where the sign over hell reads, "Abandon hope, all ye who enter here."

The effect has been disastrous, not only for individual Christians, but also for the message of the gospel as a whole. People aren't exactly ripping the roofs off churches to get inside. We see the enemy's ploy: drain all the life and beauty and adventure away from the gospel, bury Christians in duty, and nobody will want to take a closer look. It's so very unappealing.

THE DANGER OF DISOWNED DESIRE

Jenny fell in love in Ecuador. She wasn't looking for love, mind you. She had gone to South America on a missions trip. Her heart has long been devoted to bringing the gospel to Third World peoples, and frankly, she can be pretty intense about it. With her focus on the mission at hand, love was the last thing on her mind. It came as a great surprise. Perhaps it was the romance of being in a foreign country. The beauty of the mountains and the jungles, the exotic flowers and birds, and the intrigues of a Latin culture certainly provided a lush setting for romance to blossom. And then there was the fact that the man she was with was charming and intelligent and just a little bit dashing. Moreover, he was interested in her. His sincere questions, their shared laughter, a mutual sense of purpose added to the powerful potion. Jenny didn't mind at all that he was Latino; in fact, it added to the attraction. There was only one small problem: he was married.

It was with a deep sense of shame that Jenny told me her story. Nothing happened between them, but she let her heart go farther than it should. She was embarrassed, humiliated. I wasn't in the least surprised, not because Jenny is a flirt—far from it. But I've known her for a while now, and I know the story of her heart. Jenny is afraid of intimacy, and she has tried hard to live beyond her longing for love. She has known the betrayal of love and carries the wounds to prove it. Of course, she enjoyed his attention. We were made for that, remember? Like all of us, Jenny is designed for intimacy and adventure. What made me mad was that she was about to draw the wrong conclusion, a conclusion the church has long jumped to: desire gets me into trouble; I must avoid it at all costs. Jenny's story is not about the dangers of desire, but about the dangers of *disowned* desire. Just because she pretends she doesn't really want romance doesn't make the desire go away. It goes underground, to surface somewhere else at some other time.

David Whyte calls this the "devouring animal of our disowned desire." It is the reason behind most affairs in the church. The pastor lives out of duty, trying to deny his thirst for many years. One day, the young secretary smiles at him and it's over. Because he has so long been out of touch with his desire, it becomes overwhelming when it does show up. The danger of disowning desire is that it sets us up for a fall. We are unable to distinguish real life from a tempting imitation. We are fooled by the impostors. Eventually, we find some means of procuring a taste of the life we were meant for.

The sea lion was not entirely alone in those parts. For it was there he met the tortoise. Now this tortoise was an ancient creature, so weathered by his life in the barren lands that at first, the sea lion mistook him for a rock. He told the tortoise of his plight, hoping that this wise one might be able to help him. "Perhaps," the tortoise mused, "this is the sea." His eyes appeared to be shut against the bright sun, but he was watching the sea lion very closely. The sea lion swept his flippers once against his side, gliding to the end of the water hole and back. "I don't know," he said. "It isn't very deep." "Isn't it?" "Somehow, I thought the sea would be broader, deeper. At least, I hoped so."

"You must learn to be happy here," the tortoise told him one day. "For it is unlikely you shall ever find this sea of yours." Deep in his old and shriveled heart, the tortoise envied the sea lion and his sea. "But I belong to the sea. We are made for each other." "Perhaps. But you have been gone so long now, the sea has probably forgotten you." This thought had never occurred to the sea lion. But it was true, he had been gone for a long, long time. "If this is not my home, how can I ever feel at home here?" the sea lion asked. "You will, in time." The tortoise appeared to be squinting, his eyes a thin slit. "I have seen the sea, and it is no better than what you have found here." "You have seen the sea!" "Yes. Come closer," whispered the tortoise, "and I will tell you a secret. I am not a tortoise. I am a sea turtle. But I left the sea of my own accord, many years ago, in search of better things. If you stay with me, I will tell you stories of my adventures."

The stories of the ancient tortoise were enchanting and soon cast their spell upon the sea lion. As weeks passed into months, his memory of the sea faded. "The desert," whispered the tortoise, "is all that is, or was, or ever will be." When the sun grew fierce and burned his skin, the sea lion would hide in the shade of the tree, listening to the tales woven by the tortoise. When the dry winds cracked his flippers and filled his eyes with dust, the sea lion would retreat to the water hole. And so the sea lion remained, living his days between water hole and tree. The sea no longer filled his dreams.

CHAPTER FIVE

MOCKING
OUR DESIRE—
THE IMPOSTORS

*We have sailed too close to shore; having fallen in love with
life, we have lost our thirst for the waters of Life.*
—Sir Francis Drake

*And my desires, like fell and cruel hounds,
E'er since pursue me.*
—Shakespeare

The problem with desire is, you want everything.
—Paul Simon

I n fourteen hundred and ninety-two, as we all remember,
Columbus sailed the ocean blue. Instead of opening a trade
route to Asia, he unleashed something in the European imagination when he reported discovering a New World. What followed is simply amazing. First, it was the Fountain of Youth.
Ponce de León (who sailed with Columbus on his second voyage
to the Caribbean) learned from the natives of a mythical island
called Bimini. A spring was reported to flow there, whose waters
bestowed eternal youth. He actually obtained the backing of
King Ferdinand to lead a party in search of that coveted fount.

Failing to discover Bimini, Ponce de León stumbled upon Florida, which many aging Americans apparently have found to be nearly as good. Unfortunately, Ponce de León's own life was cut short by the discovery. Apparently, the natives didn't take to his attempt at conquest (and the future prospect of mobile home parks), so they killed him.

Then came El Dorado, the Lost City of Gold. As conquistadores penetrated the mainland of Central and South America, they were enchanted by a legend telling of a kingdom of unfathomable riches located somewhere in the Americas. The finder of this hidden treasure would become wealthy beyond his wildest dreams. In 1535, Sebastian de Belalcazar led a three-year search for the fabled city through the jungles of Colombia. He failed, lost control of Peru, and died of fever. You'd think his fate would have cast a chill on the whole enterprise. Not at all.

Two years later, Francisco de Orellana led an expedition down the Amazon, which also ended in disaster. About the same time, Coronado and his soldiers were marching into northern Mexico, searching for the Seven Cities of Cibola (reputed to be flowing with gold). They returned empty-handed. After a number of additional Spanish failures, Sir Walter Raleigh decided he'd give it a go. Not once, but twice he came in search of El Dorado. On his second expedition in 1616, he violated the express orders of King James I of England and attacked a Spanish settlement in Guyana. His son was killed, and Raleigh was beheaded upon his return to England.

THE SEARCH CONTINUES

What *was* it with those guys? If only Raleigh had given up on his first disappointment. But something in us will not be daunted once we've smelled the promised land. I was supposed to be writing last night, but instead sat on the couch thumbing through a Williams-Sonoma catalog. It calls itself "a catalog for cooks," but really, it's a catalog of the life we wish we had. Everything is beautiful, delicious, elegant. The kitchens portrayed are immaculate—there are no messes. Cooking there would be a joy. The tables are sumptuous with their beautiful china place settings, wine glasses brimming with nectar, gourmet foods deliciously prepared, invitingly presented. Fresh flowers abound. The homes are lovely and spacious; the view out the windows is always a mountain lake, a beach, or perhaps an English garden. Everything is as it ought to be. Glancing through its pages, you get a sense of rest. Life is good. *You see*, the images whisper, *it can be done. Life is within your grasp*. And so the quest continues. But of course. Our address used to be Paradise, remember?

And oh, how we yearn for another shot at it. Flip with me for a moment through the photo album of your heart, and collect a few of your most treasured memories. Recall a time in your life when you felt really special, a time when you *knew* you were loved. The day you got engaged perhaps. Or a childhood Christmas. Maybe a time with your grandparents. I remember one birthday in particular. My wife planned a surprise party and kept it a perfect secret. All day long, I thought everyone had forgotten me; I was thoroughly depressed. I have a hard time with birthdays anyway—the longings they rouse. I had pretty much killed my desire for something special by evening when we went to dinner at one of our favorite restaurants. There were all my friends. I was stunned, humbled, delighted all at once. It was a wonderful evening of laughter and conversation—for me, to celebrate me. A simple event, but I recall the feelings I had even still.

Hold your memory while you gather another, a time of real adventure, such as when you first learned to ride a bike, or galloped on a horse, or perhaps did something exciting on a vacation.

Stasi and I spent our tenth anniversary snorkeling in Kauai, off the Na Pali Coast. We tried to catch up to the sea turtles and grab their flippers, hoping for a ride. It was exotic and more than a little funny. I remember falling asleep that night to the sound of the waves. Now, we were meant to live in a world like that— every day. Just as our lungs are made to breathe oxygen, our souls are designed to flourish in an atmosphere rich in love and meaning, security and significance, *intimacy* and *adventure*. But we don't live in that world anymore. Far from it. Though we try to resolve the dilemma by disowning our desire, it doesn't work. It is the soul's equivalent of holding our breath. Eventually, we find ourselves gasping for air. As Allender said, "Can any human being live with a loss of soul—a loss of his or her very essence?" Of course not. Something will come along and touch those essential places in us, offering a taste of intimacy or adventure.

LOOKING FOR THE GOLDEN PERSON

"Love can touch us one time and last for a lifetime." You had to have been hibernating to have missed Celine Dion singing the theme song of *Titanic* at least once in 1998. It played constantly, in grocery stores, over the radio, and on more than nine million copies of the best-selling CD. A hauntingly beautiful song to be sure, with its Celtic strains, and made all the more powerful by the central myth of our day. Though I believe the film's success was due to its remarkable parallels to the gospel—to our longing for heroic intimacy—that is not why millions were *consciously* drawn to it. *Titanic* roused our desire for Eden, then reaffirmed the leading alternative. It offered romantic love as the answer to the heart's deepest yearnings. The idea is that someone is out there for you, and if you can find him, his love will carry you for a lifetime. How many women in particular were fueled by this film in their search for the Golden Person, their own Jack? As C. S. Lewis warned, "Another personality can become to us 'our America, our New-found-land.'"

You don't think you've been immune to all this, do you? Culture has been chanting that mantra for a long time. Of all the films, songs, television shows, musicals, dramas, poetry, and novels you've partaken of in your life, can you name more than five in which human love is *not* held up as the pinnacle of our quest? It's done so often, we don't give it a second thought when Paradise is relocated in the ideal lover. *Romeo and Juliet; Casablanca; Phantom of the Opera; The Sound of Music; Cinderella; Out of Africa; Forrest Gump.* How many couples came to the altar (or dream of coming) with this expectation? "And they all lived happily ever after." We've been fed this from childhood. Please understand me—of course, we long to be loved by another person. "It is not good for man to be alone." Most people live incredibly lonely lives. Our worst pain comes from our ever-present isolation. We are surrounded by people, but truly known by so few—if any. How we long for a soul-to-soul connection. But something else is going on here, something at the level of *worship.*

Not long ago I received a letter from a woman whose husband had left her. Having been married for ten years, she was understandably devastated. My heart broke as she poured out the pain of her divorce. But as I read on, I became more and more concerned. She said she was weeping constantly and shaking uncontrollably. She wanted to die and was seriously considering taking her own life. It was not initial shock; the letter was penned many months after their breakup. Grief is an expected and appropriate response to the loss of love. But she was reacting as though she had lost her *life.* Which is, of course, what happens when you make someone else your life.

Shortly after that, a young man whom I hadn't spoken with for a number of years called. Through his sobs, I gathered that his wife had left him and the children. He explained that she'd "met someone" on the Internet, and their relationship became her obsession. "It's my turn for love," she declared, "and I'm taking it."

If we could get some distance from it, we'd see it's no less crazy than the search for El Dorado or the Fountain of Youth. Cyber relationships have launched the search for the golden man or woman to a new level because the mystique can be maintained much longer. Internet love doesn't ever have bad breath, you don't get an STD from a terminal, and no one ever has to know. Most people don't take their search to adultery. Instead, they find other, "safer" ways to taste idyllic intimacy. It may be as subtle as that second glance or maybe never quite giving up those letters from a high school sweetheart. When that's not enough, pornography becomes the next level for men. Most women go to fantasy, fed by romance novels, soap operas, or films such as *Titanic*. How else are we to explain our revolving-door marriage policy? *It's out there*, we are told, and like those earlier explorers, we'll destroy families, homes, and careers to get it.

The potion becomes intoxicating the more openly sexual it gets. Sarah McLachlan sings in "Elsewhere,"

> I am drunk in my desire,
> I love the way your hands reach out and hold me near,
> I believe, I believe this is heaven.

You might have seen *City of Angels*, another film released in the late '90s. It tells the story of how one celestial being chooses to fall from grace into the arms of a mortal woman, who happens to be Meg Ryan. While going about his angelic duties, the angel, played by Nicolas Cage, encounters Ryan. He discovers that paradise is not where you'd expect an angel to find it (in paradise) but in her embrace. Renouncing eternity, he becomes a mortal, and they share one exquisite night together. The next morning, Ryan is killed by a bus. Even still, Cage decides it was worth it. He'd do it all again, forfeit heaven "for one smell of her perfume, one touch of her hair." It's a beautiful, powerful story, and we leave the theater with the sound track still playing in our minds, a song called "Iris" by the Goo Goo Dolls.

> And I'd give up forever to touch you,
> 'Cause I know that you feel me somehow,
> You're the closest to heaven that I'll ever be.

Sexual ecstasy has long been the leading rival to the Sacred Romance, but never has it been worshiped so blatantly. Allow me one more example.

> One dark night,
> fired with love's urgent longings
> —ah, the sheer grace!—
> I went out unseen
> my house being now stilled.
> On that glad night
> in secret, for no one saw me,
> nor did I look at anything
> with no other light or guide
> than the one that burned in my heart.
> This guided me
> more surely than the light of noon
> to where he was waiting for me
> —him I knew so well—

> there in a place where no one appeared.
> O guiding night!
> O night more lovely than the dawn!
> O night that has united
> the Lover with his beloved,
> transforming the beloved in her Lover.
> Upon my flowering breast,
> which I kept wholly for him alone

No, this is not a recent pop hit. Nor is it the theme to yet another film celebrating human love. It is taken from *The Dark Night*, penned by St. John of the Cross in the 1500s. The Lover in the poem is God, and St. John the beloved. The passion and ecstasy expressed here by this Christian mystic come from a long tradition that finds its roots in Scripture. The psalmists sang, "My soul thirsts for you, my body longs for you. Your love is better than life, my soul clings to you. Whom have I in heaven but you? And earth has nothing I desire besides you." How far we have come. Loreena McKennitt released a CD containing a song of St. John's *Dark Night*—rewritten to adore an earthly lover. She admits that St. John wrote it to "his god" (notice the small *g*), but like all of us, she chooses another god. "How skilled you are at pursuing love!" God laments. "You have lived as a prostitute with many lovers" (Jer. 2:33; 3:1 NIV).

REACHING FOR THE GOLDEN MOMENT

We do the same thing with our hunger for adventure. I imagine there must have been great excitement at the outset for those early explorers—that is, before the mosquitoes and hostile natives became realities. Most of us are not so daring; we prefer our adventure on a more modest scale. Shopping, if you can believe it, has become for most people their experience of a sort of conquest. What do you make of the credit card debt in the U.S.? More than 1.5 billion cards in circulation, with an average balance of $5,000 on each card. (How do you explain *your* current balance?)

We say we worship money, but it's not that simple. Money is merely the means to get what we really want—clothes that give us an image of attractiveness, equipment to provide excitement. Sport-utility vehicles were the top-selling line in the past ten years, but the irony is that less than 5 percent of them are ever actually taken off road. We want the illusion of adventure without really having to risk it. There is big money in outdoor gear right now; the "look" of the expedition is in. Thirty years ago you wouldn't have found a gym in every strip mall. There, in our air-conditioned sanctuaries, we tone our bodies while watching television. We'll take our adventure *vicariously*, preferring for the most part to be voyeurs of the extreme sport rage or our favorite sports teams.

I was surprised when Steven asked to see me about a problem he was having with football. He was engaged to a wonderful young woman, and things were moving along well in their relationship. "So what's wrong?" I asked. "Well . . . her dad, you see . . . he roots for the state rival of my college football team. It's kinda becoming a big deal." I had never encountered this before. This young man had a full-blown addiction to college football. He spent Monday through Friday anticipating the games, Saturday watching the games, and Sunday talking about the outcome. He knew nearly every player's name and his stats by heart. During final exams week, he tried to get away from it by securing himself in a friend's apartment with no TV. It lasted about an hour before he dialed up the Internet and picked up live coverage of his team.

As we talked about what it all meant to him, he described the thrill of going with his dad to see their team win the national play-offs. "I have a picture at home, with all of us in it—my brothers, my dad. I've never seen him so happy, so alive." Notice how important it is that it's the *home* team. We need to feel as though we are a part of the excitement.

I had an affair of my own this past summer—with an internal frame backpack. It was outrageously expensive and totally unnecessary (I have a backpack already). But still, I became obsessed. I dreamed about it during the day. At night, I pored over the catalog, comparing it with others, deepening my conviction that this was all I needed for life to be good. As Dick Keyes has pointed out, most of our idols come in pairs. There is the "nearby idol," the thing close at hand, which gives us a sense of control over our world. And then there is the "faraway idol," which provides the taste of transcendence. In my case, the backpack was the thing within reach, which promised adventure down the road. In sexuality, we work hard on our appearance (what we can control), which in turn draws others to us, bringing, we hope, a sense of being loved. The bottom line is, we don't want to wait for the promise of God to be fulfilled.

We're not the first generation to give it a go; the spirit of it goes back at least as far as the Tower of Babel. But certainly, mankind's *options* have never been greater. The technology, the finances, and the cleverness at our disposal are unsurpassed in the history of the world. The angel may be barring our way back into Eden, but we're bound and determined to get something going on our own. Wal-Mart is open twenty-four hours a day now, with a dozen restaurants nearby. Next door, a multiplex theater with thirty screens. Or stay home—we have more than a hundred channels on the TV. Then there are computer games and the Internet. We've discovered gourmet coffee (tell your grandfather you're paying five dollars for a cup), gourmet jelly beans, gourmet popcorn—you name it. We've nearly perfected our little pleasures. When the going gets tough, the tough go shopping or fishing or out to dinner. They're all impostors—every one. But we're so taken by the dizzying array of choices, we never have to stop and take a good look at what we're doing.

THE NARCOTIC OF PLEASURE

G. K. Chesterton thought that everybody ought to get drunk once a year because if that didn't do you good, the repentance in the morning would. There's nothing like waking up to what you've done, whether it's having too much to drink or eat, or letting your anger fly. The remorse after a flagrant sin often brings a sense of clarity and resolution. (How many New Year's resolutions are made the morning after?) But if we don't quite overdo it, if we keep our indulgence at a more moderate level, such clarity never comes. We never see it in black and white, for we're always under the influence. No one stops to think about it. Pleasure isn't nearly so much about true enjoyment as it is about anesthetizing ourselves. Think about the relief your idols provide: Is your desire truly and deeply satisfied, or does the relief come more through the temporary *absence* of desire?

I've had a nagging sense I was more pleasure-oriented than might be good, but I didn't see the function of pleasure in my life until I had to face intense grief and loss. I tried every drug I could, and nothing worked. Not food. Not sleep. Not work. Not reading. Not even sex. I could not get away from the pain. And then it occurred to me: If I am trying to use pleasure as a drug in this case, how many of my so-called enjoyments are merely the same thing on a lesser scale? Reading Pascal, I found he'd already hit upon the same thing. Unable to get out of the dilemma of desire, we've found a powerful drug—distraction.

> The way to render a man happy, is to engage him with an object that will make him forget his private troubles. What can be the reason that this man, who not long ago lost his only son, and this very morning was engaged almost to distraction in a law suit, now does not give his troubles a thought? You need not be astonished; he is taken up with watching a stag, which his hounds have been in full chase after, for six hours. However great his distress may have been, in this he finds ample consolation. In short, prevail upon a man to join in any amusement whatever, and as long as that lasts he will be happy; but it will be a false and imaginary happiness, arising not from the possession of real and solid good, but from a levity of spirit that obliterates the recollection of his real miseries, and fixes his thoughts upon mean and ridiculous objects, unworthy of his attention, and still less deserving of his love. (*Pensées*)

Don't be fooled by the apparent innocence of the object you've chosen. What is its *function*? Most of our idols also have a perfectly legitimate place in our lives. That's their cover. That's how we get away with our infidelity. The prophet Isaiah gives an example when he marvels at a man who cuts down a tree in the forest and then puts it to two very different uses:

> Half of the wood he burns in the fire;
> over it he prepares his meal,
> he roasts his meat and eats his fill.

Nothing wrong here. That's the perfectly appropriate use of wood. But it doesn't end here (it rarely does):

> From the rest he makes a god, his idol;
>> he bows down to it and worships.
> He prays to it and says,
>> "Save me; you are my god."

The prophet is incredulous. *Doesn't he see what he's doing?* he wonders.

> No one stops to think,
>> no one has the knowledge or understanding to say,
> "Half of it I used for fuel;
> I even baked bread over its coals,
> I roasted meat and I ate.
> Shall I make a detestable thing from what is left?
>> Shall I bow down to a block of wood?"
> He feeds on ashes, a deluded heart misleads him;
>> he cannot save himself or say,
> "Is not this thing in my right hand a lie?"
>> (Isa. 44:16–17, 19–20 NIV)

So there you have it: no one stops to think. We don't want to take a good, hard look at what we are really doing, for then we might see the lie. We would expose the impostors. We would see the water hole for the muddy puddle it is. Our idols become the *means* by which we forget who we truly are and where we truly come from. They numb us. Like Hansel and Gretel, we're following a sugared path to our destruction. Or perhaps it's the Pied Piper who's got us skipping along. (There's a reason we used to tell those fairy tales. They contained wisdom we desperately need.) How else can we explain our apparent happiness when we are so far from home? Pascal observed,

Mankind, unable to escape death, trouble and ignorance, in order to make themselves happy, have hit upon the plan of never thinking about these things; the utmost efforts of their ingenuity can suggest no better consolation for such prodigious evils. But it is most miserable consolation, since it does not cure the evil, but merely to conceal it a little while; and by concealing it, prevents men from attempting to obtain a thorough cure. (*Pensées*)

THE ASSAULT ON OUR DESIRE

The battle of desire is not something that just takes place within us or even between us. It is also taking place *against* us, all the time. Our desire is under nearly constant attack. "We come into the world longing," says Gil Bailie, "for we know not what. We *are* desire. And desire is good, for it's what takes us to God. But our desire is not hard-wired to God."

We look to others to teach us what to desire. We are intensely imitative creatures, as Aristotle pointed out. It is how we learn language; it is how we master just about anything in life. It is also how we come to seize upon the objects of our desire. We all know this, though we don't like to admit it.

One example should suffice. I was at a garage sale, looking for some tools. There was a table saw at a wonderful price. Another fellow was sort of browsing around, standing in front of the saw but not seeming particularly interested. I opened my mouth and made the fatal error: "Wow, that's a great price on that saw." You know what happened next. Immediately, his nonchalance became intense interest, and since he was there before me, he drove off with a table saw that five minutes earlier he couldn't have given two hoots about.

Madison Avenue plays on this with a cynical brilliance. Look at fashion, for example. It lives on this dynamic. We don't wear what we want to wear; we wear what everyone else is wearing this year. The new line of cars that rolls out each year survives on this as well. Do we really imagine there's a significant difference in the actual car itself? Or notice what happens every Christmas. Quite often one toy emerges as the "must have" toy. A few years ago it was a little doll called Tickle Me Elmo, after the Sesame Street character. There was a rush on the doll. Suppliers ran out. People went mad, paying hundreds and thousands of dollars to get their hands on a little red character that retails for $29.99. Incidentally, you can go to the store tomorrow and get as many as you'd like. The mimetic fever is over—or has changed focus.

Advertisers play on this constantly, urging us to desire this and that by creating the image that "everyone who is anyone" has the object for sale, and we are surely a loser if we don't join the frenzy. Sadly, the ploy works. Bailie perceives that

> we live in a world inundated by these mimetic passions. What we call "modernity" is a world of feverishly mimetic desires and fascinations. With powers of telecommunication of which the Aztecs could not have dreamed, we are given models to emulate incessantly. We are inspired to envy, desire, compete, resent, aspire and be ambitious. (*Violence Unveiled*)

The constant effort to arouse our desire and capture it can be described only as an assault. From the time we get up to the time we go to bed, we are inundated with one underlying message: *it can be done.* The life you are longing for *can* be achieved. Only buy this product, see this movie, drive this car, take this vacation, join this gym, what have you. The only disagreement is over the means, but everyone agrees on the end: we can find life now.

I suppose the architects of Madison Avenue are for the most part motivated merely by success. It's their job to sell. But behind the whole mimetic madness is an even more brilliant schemer. The evil one has basically two ploys. If he cannot get us to kill our hearts and bury our desire, then he is delighted to seduce our desire into a trap. Once we give over our desire for life to any object other than God, we become ensnared. Think of the phrase, "She's a slave to fashion." We become slaves to any number of things, which at the outset we thought would serve us. In this light, repression of desire is a much less dangerous stage in the process. Addiction is far worse, for as May explains,

> Our addictions are our own worst enemies. They enslave us with chains that are of our own making and yet that, paradoxically, are virtually beyond our control. Addiction also makes idolaters of us all, because it forces us to worship these objects of attachment, thereby preventing us from truly, freely loving God and one another. (*Addiction and Grace*)

Like the rich young ruler, we find we cannot give up our treasured possessions, whatever they may be, even though God himself is standing before us with a better offer. If you think his sad story is not also your own, you are out of touch with yourself. I remember standing in the East River several summers ago. It was a gorgeous summer evening, and I was about to enjoy some great fly-fishing. I had just begun to cast when God spoke to me. *Put down the rod,* he said. *I'd like to spend some time with you.* I was irritated. *Now?* I replied. *You want to talk to me now? Why not later on the drive home? There's plenty of time in the car.* Good grief. What an addict I am! Thus the father of lies turns our most precious treasure—our longing for God and for his kingdom—into our worst enemy. It is truly diabolical. We wind up serving our desire slavishly or resenting it, or a little of both.

OUR TIMING IS OFF

"And envy."

It was three days after Brent's fall, and I was talking to a mutual friend of ours on the phone, telling him what I had been feeling—anger, rage, grief, numbness, exhaustion. Dan said, "And envy." He went on to describe his own feelings of a sort of jealousy, that Brent was home, that he had moved "from the battle to the banquet." I didn't reply. I didn't know what to say. I wasn't feeling envy; it hadn't even crossed my mind. Certainly, part of that can be written off to what I was going through. But not all of it.

Dan's comment exposed my basic commitment to find life here and now. It is a commitment nearly all of us share, at a far deeper level than we'd like to admit. There's something just a little hurt and angry in all of us as we find that life is not coming through. A song by Don Henley called "The End of the Innocence" captures the relation between our heartache and our use of pleasure in a very sad sort of way. The opening lines go like this:

> Remember when the days were long
> And rolled beneath a deep blue sky
> Didn't have a care in the world
> With mommy and daddy standin' by
> But "happily ever after" fails
> And we've been poisoned by these fairy tales
> The lawyers clean up all details
> Since daddy had to fly

The man in the song lost the love he was meant to know as a boy when his parents divorced. It was the end of the innocence for him, his personal encounter with life after the Fall. Hurt and angry, he searches for something now to give at least a taste of

what was meant to be. Like so many men, he chooses sexual intimacy as his impostor.

> But I know a place where we can go
> Still untouched by man . . .
> So lay your head back on the ground
> Let your hair fall all round
> Offer up your best defense
> But this is the end of the innocence

Have we really been poisoned by fairy tales? No, we've
merely gotten the timing wrong. Although our desire has taken
us to a thousand "other lovers," we must not make a fatal error
and try one more time to get rid of it. We cannot revert to killing
our hearts. Instead, we must accept the first lesson in the journey
of desire: ecstasy is *not* an option. We must have life. The only
problem is in our refusal to wait. That is why God must rescue us
from the very things we thought would save us.

———

It was in May that the winds began to blow. The sea lion had grown used to wind, and at first he did not pay much heed at all. Years of desert life had taught him to turn his back in the direction from which the wind came and cover his eyes with his flippers, so that the dust would not get in. Eventually, the winds would always pass.

But not this time. Day and night it came, howling across the barren lands. There was nothing to stop its fury, nothing to even slow it down. For forty days and forty nights the wind blew. And then, just as suddenly as it had begun, it stopped. The sea lion lifted himself to have a look around. He could hardly believe his eyes.

Every single leaf had been stripped from his tree. The branches that remained, with only a twig or two upon them, looked like an old scarecrow. And I do not need to tell you that there was no longer any shade in which to hide. But worse than this, much worse indeed, was what the sea lion saw next. The water hole was completely dry.

———

CHAPTER SIX

THE DIVINE THWARTER

Someone has altered the script.
My lines have been changed . . .
I thought I was writing this play.

—*Madeleine L'Engle*

I can't get no satisfaction.

—*The Rolling Stones*

Devise your plan. It will be thwarted.

—*God*

It started five years ago with my annual fishing trip. Those of you unfamiliar with *fly*-fishing must rid your minds of the images of that other kind—guys in their lawn chairs down at the city pond, chugging cheap beer while they attempt to fool fish with fluorescent pink, garlic-flavored cheese balls beneath an enormous bobber. You wonder if they haven't met their match. To compare that with a day on a high mountain stream pursuing wild trout through the elegance and serenity of fly-fishing is like comparing the mini mart at your gas station to Nordstrom's, or professional wrestling to gymnastics, or the Simpsons to Shakespeare. Enough said.

This yearly pilgrimage has always been for me a time of consummate pleasure, a banquet of beauty with deep friendship and adventure. Then it all began to unravel. I had scheduled a few days on the Frying Pan River in Colorado in late May. The fishing there is legendary, and recent reports had been phenomenal. But as a friend and I drove up to the river, it began to rain. *Not to worry*, I thought. *Late spring often brings rain. It'll blow over in an hour or two.* As we climbed into the mountains, the rain turned into a snowstorm that lasted the entire trip.

I began to play chess with God. The following year, I planned our trip for July to eliminate all possibility of snow. I booked several days at a private ranch that caters to fly fishermen, with a guide to take us out on the upper Rio Grande. The night before we were to leave, I received a call telling me that no, it had not snowed, but thunderstorms had created mudslides and the fishing was impossible. They offered to refund my money.

I sensed that God had made a countermove, and that my king was in danger. Grabbing my phone book, I found the number of another guide on a different river and called him. Yes, the fishing was fabulous. Yes, he could take us out tomorrow. I hung up the phone with a smile. Your move, God. When we arrived early the next morning, the fellow told us sadly, "It's the strangest thing, but they opened the dam last night and the river's flooded. Sorry 'bout that."

The next year it was a drought; the year after that we still don't know what happened. High in the meadows of the Eastern Sierra, the fish had seemed to simply vanish from the San Joaquin. I was losing the game, as you can tell. But I hadn't been cornered; not yet.

Last year I was invited to speak at a conference near Bend, Oregon. It is a place very dear to me, full of memories from my childhood. The Deschutes River flows through there, and I was looking forward (can you believe my tenacity?) to some great time on the water with my new fly rod. (Country musicians use a *fiddle*, but to play Mozart, you use a *violin*. Bait fishermen use *poles*, while fly fishermen use *rods*.) I made what I felt would be my winning move. A friend arranged access for me to a private stretch of the Deschutes, a ranch visited each year by only a handful of people. The caretaker was an old master fly fisherman. When the owner of the shop in town learned where I was headed, he looked around furtively, leaned across the counter, and whispered, "Mister, that may be the best one hundred yards of fishing in the United States." Something smiled in my heart and said, *Check*.

Old Bill was a marvelous fisherman, and as we walked down to the water, he realized, "I'm thinkin' . . . let's see . . . you're the first guy to fish this since last October." *Six months ago*, I thought. *This is going to be incredible*. You know what's coming next. Nothing. We caught nothing. Bill had a funny look on his face. "John," he said, "people come from all over the world to fish this ranch. I've never had a day like this . . . ever." Feeling for all the world like Jonah, I said, "Bill, this is not about you. The fishing will be great tomorrow after I've gone." Checkmate.

CRUEL OR KIND?

This is the point at which God most feels like our enemy. It seems at times that he will go to any length to thwart the very thing we most deeply want. We can't get a job. Our attempt to find a spouse never pans out. The doctors aren't able to help us with our infertility. Isn't this precisely the reason we fear to desire in the first place? Life is hard enough as it is, but to think that God himself is working against us is more than disheartening. Job cried out, "What do you gain by oppressing me? . . . You hunt me like a lion and display your awesome power against me" (10:3, 16 NLT).

I want to state very clearly that not every trial in life is specially arranged for us by God. Much of the heartache we know comes from living in a broken world filled with broken people. And we have an enemy in the evil one who hates us deeply. But there are times when God himself seems to be set *against* us. Unless we understand our desperate hearts and our incredible tenacity to arrange for the life we want, these events will just seem cruel.

When we lived in Eden, there was virtually no restriction on the pleasure around us. We could eat *freely* from any tree in the Garden. Our desire was innocent and fully satisfied. I cannot even imagine what five minutes in total bliss would be like. We had it all, but we threw it away. By mistrusting God's heart, by reaching to take control of what we wanted, Adam and Eve set in motion a process in our hearts, a desperate grasping that can be described only as *addiction*. Desire goes mad within us. May observes, "Once they gave in to that temptation, their freedom was invaded by attachment. They experienced the need for more. God knew that they would not—*could not*—stop with just the one tree."

Our first parents are banished from Paradise as an act of mercy. The thought of the human race gaining immortality— eating from the Tree of Life—in a fallen state is too horrible to imagine. We would be evil forever. And though we are sent from the Garden, "the story of Eden is not over." Every day we reenact the Fall as we turn in our desire to the very things that will destroy us. As May reminds us,

> Addiction exists wherever persons are internally compelled to give energy to things that are not their true desires. To define it directly, addiction is a state of compulsion, obsession, or preoccupation that enslaves a person's will and desire. Addiction side-

tracks and eclipses the energy of our deepest, truest desire for love and goodness. We succumb because the energy of our desire becomes attached, nailed, to specific behaviors, objects or people. (*Addiction and Grace*)

Addiction may seem too strong a term to some of you. The woman who is serving so faithfully at church—surely, there's nothing wrong with that. And who can blame the man who stays long at the office to provide for his family? Sure, you may look forward to the next meal more than most people do, and your hobbies can be a nuisance sometimes, but to call any of this an addiction seems to stretch the word a bit too far.

I have one simple response: give it up. If you don't think you're a chess player, too, then prove it by letting go of the things that provide you with a sense of security, or comfort, or excitement, or relief. You will soon discover the tentacles of attachment deep in your soul. There will be an anxiousness; you'll begin to think about work or food or golf even more. Withdrawal will set in. If you can make it a week or two out of sheer willpower, you will find a sadness growing in your soul, a deep sense of loss. Lethargy and a lack of motivation follow.

Remember, we will make an idol of anything, especially a good thing. So distant now from Eden, we are *desperate* for life, and we come to believe that we must arrange for it as best we can, or no one will. God must thwart us to save us.

FUTILITY AND FAILURE

Adam and Eve stand before God with nothing but fig leaves to hide their shame. Knowing what has happened in our hearts, what desire can and will do divorced from its true source of happiness, God moves to intervene. With deep wisdom and kindness, he curses our lives. To Adam—and all his sons after him—God says,

> Because you listened to your wife and ate the fruit I told you not to eat, I have placed a curse on the ground. All your life you will struggle to scratch a living from it. It will grow thorns and this-tles for you, though you will eat of its grains. All your life you will sweat to produce food, until your dying day. (Gen. 3:17–19 NLT)

God thwarts men where it hurts most—in the field. He strikes a blow in the arena of our labor, our strength. This is our most vulnerable spot. We draw our sense of worth from it. I am not minimizing the importance of intimacy to a man; not at all. But when men get together, they don't talk about how everyone's relationship is doing. "Did you hear about Sally and Bill? I won-der if everything's okay. Maybe we should give them a call." No, they talk about their *achievements* (typically with a little embel-lishment). "I bagged the Zonax account today. Yep. Won't be long now before I'm running Sales." A man's impostors are most often born out of this place in his heart. Either they offer a false sense of strength, or they relieve a man from having to be strong. Pornography, for example, does both. The woman says, "I will make you feel like a man by giving myself to you, and you don't have to do anything at all. You can have the pleasure of a woman without having to *live* with her." A man's deepest desires always relate to his strength, one way or another, and so the curse for a man strikes him at the core.

As Dan Allender has pointed out, this is obviously about more than literal thorns and thistles, or every man who is not a farmer gets to escape the curse. Those who live in an apartment and work on Wall Street would get off scot-free. If only it were that easy. If only our worst enemy were dandelions and crabgrass. But every man knows the reality of the curse because every man must face the ongoing frustration of *futility* and *failure*. No matter how much a man achieves, it is never enough. He has to go out tomorrow and do it all again. If you hit a home run in last week's game, there is such a short time of joy. Next time you're at the plate, everyone expects you to do it again. And again. Futility. And even if you do seem to beat the odds and secure yourself financially, the curse is waiting for you somewhere else in your life—in your marriage or with your children. That is why a man's worst fear is not measuring up. A woman isn't affected by defeat the way a man is. It may hurt, but typically, she bounces back from failure. Not so for a man; in some cases, failure can be debilitating for life.

LONELINESS AND HEARTACHE

When God turns to the issues of a woman's wayward heart, he brings a very different curse. To Eve and all her daughters, he says, "You will bear children with intense pain and suffering. And though your desire will be for your husband, he will be your master" (Gen. 3:16 NLT).

This is obviously about more than babies and marriage, or every single woman without children gets to escape the curse. Some of our dearest friends are in that situation, and I can tell you that they do not live in Paradise. Every woman knows the reality of the curse because every woman lives with *relational heartache* and *loneliness*. With the skill of a surgeon going after a cancer, God thwarts a woman where it matters most—in her relationships. Are not her deepest tears shed over issues of failed intimacy? When women get together, they don't talk about work, unless it's to talk about their work *relationships*. This observation is not condescending in the least. A woman's glory is her heart for others, her keen sense of interpersonal dynamics, her commitment to maintaining relational connections. A woman who knows she is deeply loved typically survives a career setback that would send a man into a tailspin.

A woman's impostors are nearly always an attempt to somehow fill that ache for love or pretend she doesn't need love. The feminist movement has tried hard to assert that women can be as tough as men; they, too, can compete, can achieve, can conquer. It's tired and overdone. Like Lady Macbeth, it was an attempt by certain women to deal with the dilemma of their desire by "unsexing" themselves. Such contempt for tenderness and vulnerability reveals only how much they fear both, how deeply they have been hurt in that place. In a backhanded way, it confirms their design.

The worst fear for a woman is *abandonment*. Like a man who refuses to play the man for fear of failing, a woman who shuns intimacy only reveals her fear of rejection by refusing to face it honestly, openly. As for the love substitutes, men aren't buying Danielle Steel romances. They have to be dragged to the next "love finally finds her" movie. Women often create colorful fantasy worlds, a kind of pornography that guarantees rich intimacy in spite of the emptiness of daily life. The writers of soaps know this tendency only too well.

THE HARDEST LESSON TO LEARN

God *promises* every man futility and failure; he *guarantees* every woman relational heartache and loneliness. We spend most of our waking hours attempting to end-run the curse. We will fight this truth with all we've got. Sure, other people suffer defeat. Other people face loneliness. But not me. I can beat the odds. We see the neighbor's kids go off the deep end, and we make a mental note: *they didn't pray for their kids every day.* And we make praying for our kids every day part of our plan. It doesn't have to happen to us. We watch a colleague suffer a financial setback, and we make another note: *he was always a little lax with his money.* We set up a rigid budget and stick to it.

Isn't there something defensive that rises up in you at the idea that you cannot make life work out? Isn't there something just a little bit stubborn, an inner voice that says, *I can do it?* Thus Pascal writes,

> All men seek happiness. This is without exception. Whatever different means they employ, they all tend to this end . . . This is the motive of every action of every man. *But example teaches us little.* No resemblance is ever so perfect that there is not some slight difference, and hence we expect that *our* hope will not be deceived on this occasion as before. And thus, while the present never satisfies us, experience dupes us and from misfortune to misfortune leads us to death. (*Pensées*)

It can't be done. No matter how hard we try, no matter how clever our plan, we cannot arrange for the life we desire. Set the book down for a moment and ask yourself this question: Will life ever be what I so deeply want it to be, in a way that cannot be lost? This is the second lesson we must learn, and in many ways the hardest to accept. We must have life; we cannot arrange for it.

People will avoid this lesson all their days, changing their plans, their jobs, even their mates, rather than facing the truth.

> You were wearied by all your ways,
>> but you would not say, "It is hopeless."
> You found renewal of your strength,
>> and so you did not faint. (Isa. 57:10 NIV)

These are the majority of folks out there, Christian and pagan, who are still giving it a go. Yes, a smaller number have collided against failure and heartache in such a devastating way that they have come to see it can't be done, but they have faded into resignation, or bitterness, or despair. They have taken their revenge on the God who has thwarted them by killing their desire.

How do we accept that *it can't be done* with an open heart? How do we sustain desire in the face of ongoing failure and loneliness? It all depends on what we do with hope.

MISPLACED HOPE

"In this world you will have trouble." No kidding. Jesus, the master of understatement, captures in one sentence the story of our lives. He adds, "But take heart! I have overcome the world" (John 16:33 NIV). Why aren't we more encouraged? (Sometimes we'll try to *feel* encouraged when we hear a "religious" passage like this, but it never really lasts.) The reason is that we are still committed to arranging for life now. Be honest. Isn't there a disappointment when you realize that I'm not going to offer you the seven secrets of a really great life today? If I wanted to make millions, that's the book I would write. The only thing is, I would have to lie. It can't be done. Not *yet*. And that *yet* makes all the difference in the world because desire cannot live without hope. But hope in what? *For* what?

"Set your hope *fully* on the grace to be given you when Jesus Christ is revealed" (1 Peter 1:13 NIV, emphasis added). I read a passage like this, and I don't know whether to laugh or to cry. Fully? We don't even set our hope *partially* on the life to come. Not really, not in the desires of our hearts. Heaven may be coming. Great. But it's a long way off and who really knows, so I'm getting what I can now. Our search is limited only by our

finances, our options, and our morals. Those with fewer misgiv-
ings and greater financial discretion go farther with it. For most
Christians, heaven is a backup plan. Our primary work is finding
a life we can at least get a little pleasure from here. Heaven is an
investment we've made, like Treasury bonds or a retirement
account, which we're hoping will take care of us in the future
sometime, but which we do not give much thought to at present.
It's tucked away in a drawer at the back of our minds, while we
throw our immediate energies into playing the stock market.
God comes in like a corporate raider, ruining our plans as we
watch our "stocks" go into a tailspin.

"Remember how the LORD your God led you all the way in
the desert these forty years, to humble you and to test you in
order to know what was in your heart . . . He humbled you, causing you to hunger" (Deut. 8:2–3 NIV). When the Israelites left
Egypt, they headed across the Red Sea to Mount Sinai. From
there it was only about a two-week journey into the promised
land. Fourteen days turned into *forty years*. A blind camel would
have found its way sooner than that. God designed a supernatu-
rally long trail in order to deal with what was in their hearts.
During my five-year chess match with God, I often wrestled with
his reasons for thwarting me. *I am serving you faithfully, God. Why
won't you let me have this little pleasure?* Trip after trip was supernatu-
rally foiled. It felt to me so unfair, even cruel. I mean, we're talking about fishing, for heaven's sake. It's not as if I were trying to
have an affair. Or was I?

The day after my miraculous not-even-one-little-strike disaster
on the Deschutes, I was driving around the back roads of that
gorgeous country in central Oregon, looking at ranches and day-
dreaming. For years I've had a desire for a place of my own, several hundred acres with some riverfront, maybe here in Oregon.
My longing for a ranch preceded by years any thought of using

it for "ministry." No, ever since I was a child, the ranch has meant to me something else, my little heaven on earth. I rolled down the windows of my four-wheel drive and drank in the beauty and the solitude, the warmth of the sun, the sight of horses grazing in the fields, and the smell of the hay meadows. As I allowed myself to feel that quiet and long-buried desire, a sentence popped up out of my heart: *I really could be happy here without God.* It was completely unlooked for and remarkably honest. The thwarting had worked; now I could see what God was after in my heart. It all fell into place, and I simply said, *Oh . . . now I understand.*

God must take away the heaven we create, or it will become our hell. You may not think your efforts to arrange for a little of what you desire are anything like heaven on earth. I certainly didn't; not, at least, in the more conscious regions of my heart. But some deep and tender part of us gets trapped there in those times and places where we have had a taste of the life we long for. There in the ranch lands of central Oregon, I realized that the real issue is this: I haven't wanted to be an eternal person. I've wanted to find life here somehow. And not somehow, but through golden days on western streams, with men I love. For it was there I felt most alive, most loved, most hopeful.

As I sat there in my Jeep, surrounded by the visions and aromas—horses in a field, the pine and sage—I was transported to a time long ago in my youth, with all the promise in the air of the day ahead. And I thought, *I would give anything to return to that time in my life.* It's as if the golden center of my heart is back there in those golden days, and God wants to free it from there, to bring it into the present for the future.

I returned home a different man. Not entirely healed, not fully delivered, but still, something deep in me had shifted. The arranging had begun to stop. My heart was beginning to lift its eyes beyond the horizon toward those eternal pastures. Two weeks later Brent was killed. I began to see the hand of God in all of it, preparing me for what was coming. I think at any time during those years of thwarting, had you asked me if I truly longed for eternity, I would have said yes. My answer would not have been dishonest, but it would not have been entirely true, either. George MacDonald explained the thwarting,

> Thy hand unloved its pleasure must restrain,
> Nor spoil both gift and child by lavishing too soon.
>
> *(Diary of an Old Soul)*

THE ULTIMATE BLOW

The phone just rang. A friend's father has died of a heart attack. One minute he is going about his business like all the other drivers on the road—like us—and the next minute is his last. He was sitting at a stoplight, waiting to make a turn, and suddenly, he was gone. It was just a few months ago that I received another call, from a different friend, telling me that her little brother had died of some complications that developed from a congenital defect. He was three years old. The day before he had been out in the yard, playing on the swings and laughing.

How can we possibly continue to bet on our arranging in the face of such an overwhelming enemy as death? It is beyond me. It certainly is a testimony to our unlimited capacity for denial. As Pascal observed, it is as if we are all under a spell.

> Nothing is so important to man as his own state, nothing is so formidable to him as eternity; and thus it is not natural that there should be men indifferent to the loss of their existence, and to the perils of everlasting suffering. They are quite different with

regard to all other things. They are afraid of mere trifles; they foresee them; they feel them. And this same man who spends so many days and nights in rage and despair at the loss of an office, or for some imaginary insult to his honor, is the very one who knows without anxiety and without emotion that he will lose all by death. It is a monstrous thing to see in the same heart and at the same time this sensibility to trifles and this strange insensibility to the greatest objects. It is an incomprehensible enchantment. (*Pensées*)

In the years that followed the Fall and our exile from Eden, mankind got worse and worse. Cain killed Abel; Lamech threatened to kill everybody else. The wickedness of the human heart seemed out of control and unstoppable, even by the curses. People were living for seven, eight, even nine *hundred* years. Can you imagine the arranging that one person could accomplish with that sort of time on his hands? Stubbornness seems to come with old age. Haven't you heard your grandmother sigh and say of your grandfather, "He's set in his ways"? Multiply that by a factor of eight or nine and you get the picture. So God dealt the ultimate blow. Then the Lord said, "My Spirit will not contend with man forever, for he is mortal; his days will be a hundred and twenty years" (Gen. 6:3 NIV). He cut our life short; nobody gets to pass 120. However clever we might be in our ability to conjure Paradise, we can never get around death. It is the final thwarting.

You must follow me very carefully now. We can never fully explain the reasons surrounding someone's death. We've come to accept it for the aged, and we try to console ourselves with thoughts like, *He's had a full life.* But death is *never* natural; it was not meant to be. That is why those left behind experience such excruciating pain. The agony is only worsened when the death is what we call premature, when it takes a life in full bloom, or just as the bud begins to open. Each death can begin to be understood only within the larger story God is telling. Much of that story remains for the moment a mystery.

Many people were shattered by Brent's death. I know I was. Not even on my worst enemies would I wish such pain. But I also know this: the shattering was good. Living apart from God comes naturally; all the striving and arranging is so second nature to me that to have it stopped in its tracks was a great good. I would wake in the morning in those early days of grief, and instead of my desires "rushing at me like a pack of wild animals" as Lewis said, I knew *it can't be done*. I knew it more deeply and more personally than I had ever known it before. We must learn this lesson, at whatever cost, or the spell will not be broken and we will never discover true hope.

WHAT THEN?

"There's nothing now but heaven." It was one of those truly honest moments, when my heart speaks what I most deeply believe. Stasi and I had just finished watching *A River Runs Through It*, and the warm tears rolled quietly down my face as I sat looking out the back window of our home into the night. In a subtle and unlooked-for way, the film had brought the reality of all my losses flooding back to me. The only time and place I ever really connected with my father was when we were fishing the rivers and streams of the West. But even that could not hold us together. As time passed our trips came to an end, and we drifted apart.

Years later, as a grown man, I came home distraught from a day alone on the river. I was agitated, and though I did not know why, I knew it was not because I had not caught anything. As

Stasi and I spoke about my frustration and disappointment, the words of truth slipped from my mouth: "I'll never find him out there." I hadn't known until that moment what I had been looking for in all those years of fly-fishing.

A River Runs Through It beautifully captures the author's time of boyhood innocence, and fly-fishing trips in Montana with his father, and losing it all. The story ends with the author, now an old man, standing alone in a river, fishing. "Now, all those I loved and did not understand in my youth are gone . . . But I still reach out to them." The words were true for me; they are true for all of us. It can't be done; yet the desire remains. This is the most crucial moment for our hearts. Once we come to accept that we can never find or hang on to the life we have been seeking, what then? As Dallas Willard writes, it matters for all the world to know that life is ahead of us.

> I meet many faithful Christians who, in spite of their faith, are deeply disappointed in how their lives have turned out. Sometimes it is simply a matter of how they experience aging, which they take to mean they no longer have a future. But often, due to circumstances or wrongful decisions and actions by others, what they had hoped to accomplish in life they did not . . . Much of the distress of these good people comes from a failure to realize that their life lies before them . . . the life that lies endlessly before us in the kingdom of God. (*The Divine Conspiracy*)

Pascal also observed, "We are never living, but hoping to live; and whilst we are always preparing to be happy, it is certain, we never shall be so, if we aspire to no other happiness than what can be enjoyed in this life."

Desire cannot live without hope. Yet we can only hope for

what we desire. There simply must be something more, something out there on the road ahead of us, that offers the life we
prize. To sustain the life of the heart, the life of deep desire, we
desperately need to possess a clearer picture of the life that lies
before us.

CHAPTER SEVEN

THE GREAT RESTORATION

We shall not cease from exploration
And the end of all our exploring
Will be to arrive where we started
And know the place for the first time.

—*T. S. Eliot*

Look, I am making all things new!

—Jesus of Nazareth

See! The winter is past;
*   the rains are over and gone.*
Flowers appear on the earth;
*   the season of singing has come.*

—*Song of Songs* 2:11–12 *NIV*

I was walking in the woods and fields behind our house one evening, four months after Brent's death. My heart was so aware of the loss—not only of Brent, but in some ways, of everything that mattered. I knew that one by one, I would lose everyone I cared about and the life I am still seeking. In the east, a full moon was rising, bright and beautiful and enormous as it seems when it is just above the horizon. Toward the west, the clouds were turning peach and pink against a topaz sky. Telling myself to long for eternity feels like telling myself to let go of all I love—forever. It feels like accepting the teaching of Eastern religions, a *denial* of life and all God created. We lose it all too soon, before we can begin to live and love. But what if? What if nature is speaking to us? What if sunrise and sunset tell the tale every day, remembering Eden's glory, prophesying Eden's return? What if it shall all be restored?

THE SECRET OF SPRING

Winter tarries long at six thousand feet. Here in the Rocky Mountains, spring comes late and fitfully. We had snow again last week—the second week in May. Our boys are about to get out of school for summer vacation, and it's snowing. I've come to accept that spring here is really a wrestling match between winter and summer, as if winter doesn't want to let go its grip until it absolutely has to. It makes for a long time of waiting. You see, the flowers are pretty much gone in September. The first of October, the aspens start turning gold and drop their leaves in a week or two. Come November all is gray. Initially, I don't mind. The coming of winter has its joys, and there are Thanksgiving and Christmastime to look forward to.

But after the new year, things begin to drag on. Through February and then March, the earth remains lifeless. The whole world lies shadowed in brown and gray tones, like an old photograph. Winter's novelty is long past, and by April we are longing for some sign of life—some color, some hope. Instead, we get dumped on. It's our biggest snow month. While the azaleas are coming out in full glory in Atlanta, and the dogwoods are blooming pink and white in Portland, we are shoveling several feet of snow. It's too long.

And then, just this afternoon, I rounded the corner into our neighborhood, and suddenly, the world was green again. The bluffs behind our house were transformed. What had been rock and twig and dead mulch was a rich oriental carpet of green. I was shocked, stunned. How did it happen? As if in disbelief, I got out of my car and began to walk through the woods, touching every leaf. Just yesterday the scrub oaks had the twisted, gnarled look of the hands of an old witch. Now they are beautiful, tender, supple like a maiden. The birds are back as well, waking us in the morning with their glad songs. All the chirps and cheeps and whistles and twitters, a raucous melody of simple joy. It happened suddenly. In the twinkling of an eye.

My surprise is telling. It seems natural to long for spring; it is another thing to be completely stunned by its return. I am truly and genuinely surprised, as if my reaction were, *Really? What are you doing here?* And then I realized, *I never thought I'd see you again.* I think in some deep place inside, I had accepted the fact that winter is what is really true. As I lived through the first year of my grief, I had unconsciously settled into resignation. Empty and still, the world outside seemed a confirmation, the only fitting backdrop to the world within. I am shocked by the return of spring. And I wonder, *Can the same thing happen for my soul?*

> Grief melts away
> Like snow in May
> As if there were no such cold thing.
> Who would have thought my shrivl'd heart
> Could have recover'd greennesse? It was gone
> Quite underground
>
> And now in age I bud again,
> After so many deaths I live and write;
> I once more smell the dew and rain,

And relish versing: O my only light
It cannot be
That I am he
On whom thy tempests fell all night.
("The Flower" George Herbert)

Can it really happen? Can things in our lives be green again? No matter what our creeds may tell us, our hearts have settled into another belief. We have accepted the winter of this world as the final word and tried to get on without the hope of spring. *It will never come*, we have assumed, *and so I must find whatever life here I can.* We have been so committed to arranging for our happiness that we have missed the signs of spring. We haven't given any serious thought to what might be around the corner. Were eternity to appear tomorrow, we would be as shocked as I have been with the return of spring this week, only more so. Our practical agnosticism would be revealed. Pascal declared, "Our imagination so powerfully magnifies time, by continual reflections upon it, and so diminishes eternity . . . for want of reflection, that we make a nothing of eternity and an eternity of nothing."

MORE THAN CHURCH FOREVER

But of course we aspire to happiness we can enjoy now. Our hearts have no place else to go. We have made a nothing of eternity. If I told you that your income would triple next year, and that European vacation you've wanted is just around the corner, you'd be excited, hopeful. The future would look promising. It seems possible, *desirable*. But our ideas of heaven, while possible, aren't all that desirable. Whatever it is we think is coming in the next season of our existence, we don't think it is worth getting all that excited about. We make a nothing of eternity by enlarging the significance of this life and by diminishing the reality of what the next life is all about. Nearly every Christian I have spoken with has some idea that eternity is an unending church service. After all, the Bible says that the saints "worship God in heaven," and without giving it much more thought we have settled on an image of the never-ending sing-along in the sky, one great hymn after another, forever and ever, amen.

And our heart sinks. *Forever and ever? That's it? That's the good news?* And then we sigh and feel guilty that we are not more "spiritual." We lose heart, and we turn once more to the present to find what life we can. Eternity ends up having no bearing on our search for life whatsoever. It feels like the end of the search. And since we're not all that sure about what comes after, we search hard now. Remember, *we can only hope for what we desire.* How can the church service that never ends be more desirable than the richest experiences of life here? It would be no small difference if you knew in your heart that the life you prize is just around the corner, that your deepest desires have been whispering to you all along about what's coming. You see, Scripture tells us that God has "set eternity" in our hearts (Eccl. 3:11 NIV). Where in our hearts? In our *desires.*

The return of spring brings such relief and joy and anticipation. Life has returned, and with it sunshine, warmth, color, and the long summer days of adventure together. We break out the lawn chairs and the barbecue grill. We tend the garden and drink in all the beauty. We head off for vacations. Isn't this what we most deeply long for? To leave the winter of the world behind, what Shakespeare called "the winter of our discontent," and find ourselves suddenly in the open meadows of summer?

I am standing in my hotel room, which looks like every other hotel room I've been in over the past ten years. When you travel for a living, the excitement of hotel stays wears off pretty quickly.

There is a picture on the wall, a painting of a small harbor town. It appears to be somewhere in the Mediterranean, with its azure seas and whitewashed walls. I think of the Greek islands, perhaps Santorini. Sunlight fills the place, and small boats drift lazily in the bay. There are cafes, I am sure, filled with laughter. Along the plaza, lovers stroll hand in hand. The seas are warm and inviting. It evokes a longing, but not for vacation. Vacations end. The longing evoked by the painting is for a life that never ends.

Now . . . what if spring and summer are nature's way of expressing what Jesus was in fact trying to tell us? After all, nature is God's word to us also (Rom. 1:20). If we paid close attention, we would discover something of great joy and wonder: the restoration of the world played out before us each spring and summer is *precisely* what God is promising us about our lives. Jesus preached far more than the gospel of sin management. The good news he brought was much, much greater than forgiveness. Jesus came to announce the coming of "the kingdom of God."

> Jesus went throughout Galilee, teaching in their synagogues, preaching the good news of the kingdom. (Matt. 4:23 NIV)

> The time has come . . . The kingdom of God is near. Repent and believe the good news! (Mark 1:15 NIV)

> After this, Jesus traveled about from one town and village to another, proclaiming the good news of the kingdom of God. (Luke 8:1 NIV)

> After his suffering, he showed himself to these men and gave many convincing proofs that he was alive. He appeared to them over a period of forty days and spoke about the kingdom of God. (Acts 1:3 NIV)

And what exactly is this "kingdom of God"? What does it mean for our lives? A kingdom is a realm, quite simply, where the king's word has full sway. What the king desires is what happens. God's kingdom come means that his will is done "on *earth* as it is in heaven." Now in heaven, things are not stained or broken; everything is as it was meant to be. Think for a moment of the wonder of this. Isn't every one of our sorrows on earth the result of things *not* being as they were meant to be? And so when the kingdom of God comes to earth, wonderful things begin to unfold. Look at the evidence; watch what happens to people as they are touched by the kingdom of God through Jesus. As he went about "preaching the good news of the kingdom," Jesus was also "healing every disease and sickness among the people" (Matt. 4:23 NIV). When he "spoke to them about the kingdom of God," he "healed those who needed healing" (Luke 9:11 NIV). A direct connection is being made here. The actions of Jesus are the illustrations for the sermon.

What happens when we find ourselves in the kingdom of God? The disabled jump to their feet and start doing a jig. The deaf go out and buy themselves stereo equipment. The blind are headed to the movies. The dead are not at all dead anymore, but very much alive. They show up for dinner. In other words, human brokenness in all its forms is healed. The kingdom of God brings *restoration*. Life is restored to what it was meant to be. "In the beginning," back in Eden, all of creation was pronounced good because all of creation was exactly as God meant for it to be. For it to be good again is not for it to be destroyed, but healed, renewed, brought back to its goodness.

Those glimpses we see in the miracles of Jesus were the first-fruits. When he announces the full coming of the kingdom, Jesus says, "Look, I am making *all things* new!" (Rev. 21:5 NLT, emphasis added). He does not say, "I am making all new things." He means that the things that have been so badly broken will be restored and then some. "You mean I'll get a new pair of glasses?" my son Sam asked. "Or do you mean I'll get a new pair of eyes, so I won't need glasses?" What do you think? Jesus didn't hand out crutches to help the disabled.

THE JOY OF RESTORATION

Those of you who have been miraculously healed from a serious illness or injury will be ahead of me on this. You know firsthand the wonder and joy of restoration. But most of us have not experienced something quite so dramatic (not yet). So let me use a more common illustration, something most of you will remember—the flu. Several years ago, at Christmastime, my whole family was hit with a really vicious bug. It knocked us on our backs—literally. We brought blankets and pillows downstairs into the family room because no one had it in him to make it to his bedroom. For five days all we could do was lie on the floor, moaning. We ate nothing and drank nothing. Our house looked like an infirmary. You'll remember how awful it feels—the fever, the aches, the boredom.

One by one, we began to recover. Our first drink was simply water. It tasted like a living spring. I would have sworn it was from a different tap than we'd been using all those years. We moved up to fruit juice. It was exotic, as if we had never tasted anything like it in our lives. Each "new" food was an adventure. While I was lying in misery, I was dreaming of the day we'd go down to our favorite Mexican restaurant. It was off the charts, a sensory paradise. All things were new and absolutely delightful. It was a joy just to be alive. Our bodies had been "restored."

And going outside, after being closed in for a week, was like being released from prison. I wanted to run around, do everything all at once. I can only imagine what it would be like to walk for the very first time ever. Or to have been blind all my life and then have my sight restored. Such joy, such wonder. In *Pilgrim at Tinker Creek*, Annie Dillard recounts the stories that were reported of blind men and women who received some of the first cataract operations:

> A little girl visits a garden. "She is greatly astonished, and can scarcely be persuaded to answer, stands speechless in front of the tree, which she only names on taking hold of it, and then as 'the tree with the lights in it.'" . . . One girl was eager to tell her blind friend that "men do not really look like trees at all," and astounded to discover that her every visitor had an utterly different face. Finally, a twenty-two-year-old girl was dazzled by the world's brightness and kept her eyes shut for two weeks. When at the end of that time she opened her eyes again, she did not recognize any objects, but, "the more she now directed her gaze upon everything about her, the more it could be seen how an expression of gratification and astonishment overspread her features; she repeatedly exclaimed: 'Oh God! How beautiful!'"

How beautiful indeed. Can you imagine seeing wildflowers for the first time? Gerard Manley Hopkins was right: "The world is charged with the grandeur of God." Perhaps the reason there is reported a silence for half an hour of eternity is that we are all quite speechless (Rev. 8:1). And perhaps the gratification and astonishment that swell up afterward are the chorus of worship we are told about. "Look at this! Look there at that! Oh God! How beautiful!" Even for those of us who have always enjoyed our sight, it will be as if we are seeing for the first time. T. S. Eliot wrote in "Little Gidding,"

The end of all our exploring
Will be to arrive where we started
And know the place for the first time.

OUR RESTORATION

Yes, dear friends, we are already God's children, and we can't even imagine what we will be like when Christ returns. But we do know that when he comes we will be like him, for we will see him as he really is. (1 John 3:2 NLT)

We have an expression that we use to describe someone who's out of sorts, who's not acting like the person we know her to be: "She's just not herself today." It's a marvelous, gracious phrase, for in a very real way, no one is quite himself today. There is more to us than we have seen. I know my wife is a goddess. I know she is more beautiful than she imagines. I have seen it slip out, seen moments of her glory. Suddenly, her beauty shines through, as though a veil has been lifted. It happened one night last fall.

We had slipped away from life for a long weekend in Mexico, a time to heal and rest and just be together again. We chose a hotel away from the crowds and the *turistas*. So we were almost entirely alone one evening as we ate dinner on a veranda overlooking the Sea of Cortez. Night had fallen, and the sky was so deeply black, the stars were shining right down to the horizon of the water. We sat gazing out to sea, listening to the mariachis and the breakers and our own hearts. I turned to steal a glimpse at my wife. She was beautiful, there in the moonlight, tanned from the sun, rested, serene. She was simply beautiful in a way that life often prevents her from being, but in a way she was destined to be.

All of us have moments like this, glimpses of our true creation. They come unexpectedly and then fade again. Life for the most part keeps our glory hidden, cloaked by sin, or sorrow, or merely weariness. When I see an older woman, doubled over with arthritis, the hard years etched into her face, I want to cry, *Eve, what happened?* How truly wonderful it will be to see her in her youth again, the full flower of her beauty restored.

When the disciples saw Jesus on the Mount of Transfiguration, they got a peek at his glory. He was radiant, beautiful, magnificent. He was Jesus, the Jesus they knew and loved—only *more so.* And we shall be glorious as well. Jesus called himself the Son of man to state clearly that he is what mankind was meant to be. What we see in Jesus is our personal destiny. Is this not the secret of every fairy tale? As Frederick Buechner reminds us,

> Maybe above all they are tales of transformation where all creatures are revealed in the end as what they truly are—the ugly duckling becomes a great white swan, the frog is revealed to be a prince, and the beautiful but wicked queen is unmasked in all her ugliness. They are tales of transformation where the ones who live happily ever after, as by no means everybody does in fairy tales, are transformed into what they have it in them at their best to be. (*Telling the Truth*)

I've spoken with many people who believe that we become "spirits" when we die; that we lose our bodies and float around. Some even believe we become angels. But I don't want to lose my body; I very much want it to be renewed. When we conceive of our future existence as something ghostly, mysterious, completely "other" than anything we've ever known, we place it beyond all hoping for. (You can only hope for what you desire.) The "otherness" of it takes away its power. But look at the first example—Jesus. What happens to him after he dies? He is resurrected, of course. As someone or something else? No, as himself, only healed and very much alive. Then what—float around? No, he has breakfast.

> Early in the morning, Jesus stood on the shore, but the disciples did not realize that it was Jesus. He called out to them, "Friends, haven't you any fish?" "No," they answered. He said, "Throw your net on the right side of the boat and you will find some." When they did, they were unable to haul the net in because of the large number of fish. Then the disciple whom Jesus loved said to Peter, "It is the Lord!" . . . When they landed, they saw a fire of burning coals there with fish on it, and some bread . . . Jesus said to them, "Come and have breakfast." (John 21:4–12 NIV)

Now think about this for a minute. You're the Son of God. You've just accomplished the greatest work of your life, the stunning rescue of mankind. You rose from the dead. What would you do next? Have a cookout with a few friends? It seems so unspiritual, so *ordinary*. Do you see that eternal life does not become something totally "other," but rather that life goes on—only as it should be?

Jesus did not vanish into a mystical spirituality, becoming one with the cosmic vibration. Jesus has a body, and it's *his* body. His wounds have been healed, but the scars remain—not gruesome, but lovely, a remembrance of all he did for us. His friends recognize him. They share a bite to eat. This is our future as well—our lives will be healed and we shall go on, never to taste death again. And so MacDonald writes in a letter to his wife,

> We may however say to ourselves—one day these souls of ours will blossom into the full sunshine—when all that is desirable in

the commonness of daily love, and all we long for of wonder and
mystery and the look of Christmas time will be joined in one,
and we shall walk as in a wondrous dream yet with more sense
of reality than our most waking joy now gives us. (*The Heart of
George MacDonald*)

The creation, we are told, groans for this day, the day when
we—the sons and daughters of God—are revealed for who we
truly are.

THE EARTH IS RESTORED

The creation waits in eager expectation for the sons of God to
be revealed. For the creation was subjected to frustration, not by
its own choice, but by the will of the one who subjected it, in
hope that the creation itself will be liberated from its bondage to
decay and brought into the glorious freedom of the children of
God. (Rom. 8:19–21 NIV)

The created world itself can hardly wait for what's coming next.
Everything in creation is being more or less held back. God
reins it in until both creation and all the creatures are ready and
can be released at the same moment into the glorious times
ahead. Meanwhile, the joyful anticipation deepens. (Rom.
8:19–21 *The Message*)

How wondrous this will be! Creation can be so breathtaking
now. What shall it be like when it is released to its full glory?
Reading the journals of Lewis and Clark's journey across the
West, I am filled with longing to see what they saw. The Great
Plains were filled with wildlife; the buffalo dwelled in herds of
hundreds of thousands. One of the first white men to see this
paradise, Meriwether Lewis wrote in his journal,

I ascended to the top of the cut bluff this morning, from whence I had a most delightful view of the country—immense herds of buffalo, elk, deer and antelopes feeding in one common and boundless pasture. The buffalo, elk and antelope are so gentle that we pass near them while feeding, without appearing to excite any alarm among them, and when we attract their attention, they frequently approach us more nearly to discover what we are . . . The country is beautiful in the extreme.

It was the world "with dew still on it," to use MacLean's delightful phrase. And it will be our Paradise again. We seem to have forgotten—or perhaps we've never been told—that we get the earth back as well. Too many of us have placed eternity somewhere "out there," in a wispy and ethereal "heaven" that we cannot imagine; in the clouds perhaps. "I love the earth," wrote a friend, "and it makes me sad to think it will all be destroyed one day." We have all probably shared in this sadness. But we needn't. "Behold," says the Lord, "I will create new heavens and a new earth" (Isa. 65:17; Rev. 21:1 NIV). When he says he is making all things new, he includes the earth.

But won't the earth be destroyed, and won't we all go "up" to heaven? Peter wrote some pretty ominous words about the end of this age: "That day will bring about the destruction of the heavens by fire, and the elements will melt in the heat" (2 Peter 3:12 NIV). It looks like the whole cosmos is going down in a ball of flames. But wait—by way of comparison, Peter pointed to the Flood of Noah's day as an allegory for the "day of the Lord." He said about the Flood, "By these waters also the world of that time was deluged and destroyed" (v. 6 NIV). Now, we know that the earth was *not* destroyed by the Flood. The earth remained; the ark didn't land on Mars. What was destroyed was all the wickedness and corruption of mankind (Gen. 6–7). The Flood *cleansed* the earth, renewed it. Noah stepped out with his family onto a restored earth to begin again.

Fire is also used for cleansing throughout the Scriptures. Paul declared that our life's work will be tested in the fire, like gold. Only the dross is burned away (1 Cor. 3:13–15). This is the fire Peter refers to when he says, "But the day of the Lord will come like a thief. The heavens will disappear with a roar; the elements will be destroyed by fire, and the earth and everything in it will be *laid bare*" (2 Peter 3:10 NIV, emphasis added). The meaning of the word used here is not *destroyed*, but much closer translated as *revealed*. In other words, the world will be "exposed to judgment," and the earth will be cleansed of all unrighteousness. And a good scrubbing it needs. After declaring that the earth is full of the grandeur of God, Hopkins goes on to ask why we no longer see the glory of God in it.

> Generations have trod, have trod, have trod;
>> And all is seared with trade; bleared, smeared with toil;
>> And wears man's smudge and shares man's smell: the soil
> Is bare now, nor can foot feel, being shod.

All the strip mines and strip malls, all the incredibly ugly things we've done to the earth. No wonder the fire of God's jealous love will burn; he intends to cleanse the earth, once more, once and for all. Thus John (the writer of Revelation) sees the New Jerusalem not floating in the clouds, but descending from heaven *to the earth*, and he hears "a loud voice from the throne saying, 'Now the dwelling of God is with men, and he will live with them. They will be his people, and God himself will be with them and be their God'" (21:2–3 NIV). So Dallas Willard assures us, *"The life we now have as the persons we now are will continue in the universe in which we now exist."* The earth has been our home and will be our home in eternity. This is a great consolation. When we place eternity "out there somewhere," in a place we cannot conceive of, we are left longing for home. To lose the only world we have ever known—a world so full of memories, so rich and beautiful, with so much left to explore—is to lose something deep and priceless to our hearts.

ALL SHALL BE WELL

At the end of *The Chronicles of Narnia*, Aslan seems to have brought that delightful kingdom to an end, and the children are left to mourn its loss.

"So," said Peter, "night falls on Narnia. What, Lucy! You're not *crying*? With Aslan ahead, and all of us here?" "Don't try to stop me, Peter," said Lucy, "I am sure Aslan would not. I am sure it is not wrong to mourn for Narnia. Think of all that lies dead and frozen behind that door." "Yes, and I *did* hope," said Jill, "that it might go on forever. I knew *our* world couldn't. I did think Narnia might." "Sirs," said Tirian. "The ladies do well to weep. See, I do so myself. I have seen my mother's death. What world but Narnia have I ever known? It were no virtue, but great discourtesy, if we did not mourn."

But as the children venture farther into Aslan's country, they begin to recognize every rock and stream and tree. They have been there before. And then they discover, to their wonder and joy, that Narnia exists forever in Aslan's country, that the world they loved has been preserved, though more rich and more real than ever.

It was the Unicorn who summed up what everyone was feeling. He stamped his right fore-hoof on the ground and neighed, and then cried: "I have come home at last! This is my real country! I belong here. This is the land I have been looking for all my life, though I never knew it till now. The reason why we loved the old Narnia is that it sometimes looked a little like this."

Our search for the Golden Moment is not a search in vain; not at all. We've only had the timing wrong. We do not know exactly how God will do it, but we do know this: the kingdom of God brings restoration. The only things destroyed are the things outside God's realm—sin, disease, death. But we who are God's children, the heavens and the earth he has made, will go on. "The wolf will live with the lamb, the leopard will lie down with the goat, the calf and the lion and the yearling together" (Isa. 11:6 NIV). "And Jerusalem will be known as the Desirable Place," the place of the fulfillment of all our desires (Isa. 62:12 NLT). This is significant because it touches upon the question, What will we *do* in eternity? If all we've got are halos and harps, our options are pretty limited. But to have the whole cosmos before us—wow. Thus MacDonald writes to his daughter, whom he will soon lose to tuberculosis,

I do live expecting great things in the life that is ripening for me and all mine—when we shall have all the universe for our own, and be good merry helpful children in the great house of our father. Then, darling, you and I and all will have the grand liberty wherewith Christ makes free—opening his hand to send us out like white doves to range the universe. (*The Heart of George MacDonald*)

CHAPTER EIGHT

THE GRAND AFFAIR

Thy fishes breathe but where thy waters roll;
Thy birds fly but within thy airy sea;
My soul breathes only in thy infinite soul;
I breathe, I think, I love, I live but thee.
Oh, breathe, oh, sink—O Love, live into me.
                                            —George MacDonald

Happiness can be found neither in ourselves nor in external
things, but in God and in ourselves as united to him.
                                            —Pascal

And the people came together and the people came to dance
and they danced like a wave upon the sea.
                                            —William Butler Yeats

Several years ago I gave a series of lectures on eternity to a group of career-age singles on the East Coast. Over lunch one afternoon, several of the women asked if they might have a word with me. I sensed they wanted to ask a question that they didn't feel comfortable raising during our group discussion time. After a bit of nervous hemming and hawing, they got down to the point. Though quite successful professionally, they were feeling the ache and disappointment of singleness. And as the years seemed to be racing by, they weren't feeling so young anymore. A lifetime of singleness was becoming more and more a reality for each one, though by no means her heart's desire. What I had been saying about heaven was certainly attractive, but still, they could not shake a fear that they will forever miss one of the deepest joys of human experience. "Will there be sex in heaven?" I smiled at their courage; it's a question many haven't let themselves wonder, even though they do wonder.

THE UNION THAT WE CRAVE

To understand the importance of the question, you've got to recognize the ache that seems to be met only through sexual union. When God created Eve, as you will recall, he took her straight from Adam's side. None of us have fully recovered from the surgery. There is an aloneness, an *incompleteness* that we experience every day of our lives. How often do you feel deeply and truly known? Is there another soul to whom a simple glance is all that is necessary to communicate depth of understanding? Do you have someone with whom you can commune in love? This is our inconsolable longing—to know and to be known. It is our deepest ache, which we feel to be healed only in our union with another. Even physically, there is an incompleteness until our bodies are joined together.

But let's take a closer look. What are we looking for in the opposite sex? The Beloved in Song of Songs captures something of what the heart of a woman is seeking:

> Listen! My lover!
> Look! Here he comes,
> leaping across the mountains,
> bounding over the hills.

> My lover is like a gazelle or a young stag.
> (2:8–9 NIV)

Picture the opening sequences of the film *Last of the Mohicans*. It is 1757. England is at war with France for possession of the American colonies. "Three men, the last of a vanishing people, are on the frontier west of the Hudson River." Before us is a vast panorama of untamed wilderness. Mountain and forest as far as the eye can see. The camera takes us down into those woods, and we discover the men, running at full speed through the deep forest. Leaping across ravines, bounding with grace and speed through the heavy undergrowth, they are clearly on a great mission.

This is our first glimpse of Nathaniel, the hero of the story. Raised by the Mohawk, he is rugged, wild, *alive*. Out here on the edge of the frontier, there is something dangerous about these men. But it does not make us afraid; rather, we are all the more drawn to them. No words are spoken in this scene; no words need to be spoken. It is an image of masculinity in motion. This is what has stirred the woman's heart in Songs—to see her man's strength. And she invites that strength to come to her in the night:

> Until the day breaks
> and the shadows flee,
> turn, my lover,
> and be like a gazelle
> or like a young stag
> on the rugged hills.
> (2:17 NIV)

There is an emptiness in the woman that only her man can fill. Is it not physically true? But it is more than just physically true. Our bodies are an outward sign of an inward reality. So, too, the woman completes her man in a uniquely beautiful way. Come to me, she says, and let your strength be fully expressed in the garden of my beauty. Is this not the invitation that stirs a man's heart? For these are the qualities of the Beloved that captivate her Lover in the Song. He says,

> How beautiful you are, my darling!
> Oh, how beautiful!
> Your eyes behind your veil are doves . . .
> Your lips are like a scarlet ribbon;
> your mouth is lovely . . .
> Your two breasts are like two fawns,
> like twin fawns of a gazelle
> that browse among the lilies.
>
> (4:1, 3, 5 NIV)

Shortly after the opening sequence of the *Mohicans* in the forest, we are given our first glimpse of Cora, the heroine of the film. And such a contrast to the warriors she is. Cora is British; she wears a lovely white dress, fringed with lace and flowing to the ground. Beauty and grace have come to the frontier. She wears a summer hat with a wide brim, which for a moment veils her dark eyes, rich and deep as pools of water, soft as doves. She is mysterious, but her mystery is not one that forbids. Rather, she is captivating. Her lips are red, like the Beloved in Songs, and her fitted bodice, in no way immodest, is alluring. Though an entire war party of Hurons is not enough to trap Nathaniel, he is captured by Cora's femininity, "held captive" by her long black hair, just as the Lover is in the Song.

> My lover has gone down to his garden,
> to the beds of spices,

> to browse in the gardens
>   and to gather lilies.
> I am my lover's and my lover is mine;
>   he browses among the lilies.
>
>   (6:2–3 NIV)

There is no union on earth like the consummation of the love between a man and a woman. No other connection reaches as deeply as this oneness was meant to; no other passion is nearly so intense. People don't jump off bridges because they lost a grandparent. If their friend makes another friend, they don't shoot them both. No one has ruined home and career for a rendezvous at the library. Troy didn't go down in flames because somebody lost a pet. The passion that spousal love evokes is instinctive, irrational, intense, and dare I say, immortal. As the Song says,

> Love is as strong as death,
>   its jealousy unyielding as the grave.
> It burns like a blazing fire,
>   like a mighty flame.
> Many waters cannot quench love;
>   rivers cannot wash it away.
>
>   (8:6–7 NIV)

Small wonder that many people experience sexual passion as their highest transcendence on this earth. This love surpasses all others as the source of the world's most beautiful poetry, art, and music. Lovers reach for the stars to find words fitting enough to express what the beloved means to them and still feel those words fall short. Granted, much of it is hyperbole, expressing more the dream than the reality. But that is precisely my point. It is not merely hormones and sex drives projected outward. It is a clue to a deeper reality, a reach for something that does exist. For this exotic intimacy was given to us as a picture of something else, something truly out of this world.

OUR LOVE AFFAIR WITH GOD

After creating this stunning portrait of a total union, the man and woman becoming one, God turns the universe on its head when he tells us that this is what *he* is seeking with *us*. In fact, Paul says it is *why* God created gender and sexuality and marriage—to serve as a living metaphor. He quotes Genesis, then takes it to the nth degree: "'For this reason a man will leave his father and mother and be united to his wife, and the two will become one flesh.' This is a profound mystery—but I am talking about Christ and the church" (Eph. 5:31–32 NIV).

A profound mystery indeed. All the breathtaking things in life are. The Cross is a great mystery, but we are helped in understanding it by looking back into the Old Testament and finding there the pattern of the sacrificial lamb. Those early believers did not understand the full meaning of what they were doing, but once Christ came, the whole period of ritual sacrifice was seen in a new light, and in turn gave a richer depth to our understanding of the Cross.

We must do the same with this stunning passage; we must look back and see the Bible for what it is—the greatest romance ever written. God creates mankind for intimacy with himself, as his beloved. We see it right at the start, when he gives us the highest freedom of all—the freedom to reject him. The reason is obvious: love is possible only when it is freely chosen. True love is never constrained; our hearts cannot be taken by force. So God sets out to woo his beloved and make her his queen:

I remember the devotion of your youth,
    how as a bride you loved me
and followed me through the desert,
    through a land not sown.
Israel was holy to the LORD,
    the firstfruits of his harvest;
all who devoured her were held guilty,
    and disaster overtook them.

(Jer. 2:2–3 NIV)

I gave you my solemn oath and entered into a covenant with you, declares the Sovereign LORD, and you became mine . . . I dressed you in fine linen and covered you with costly garments. I adorned you with jewelry . . . You became very beautiful and rose to be a queen. And your fame spread among the nations on account of your beauty, because the splendor I had given you made your beauty perfect. (Ezek. 16:8, 10–11, 13–14 NIV)

If you're writing a romance, love is the goal; you must allow for the possibility of betrayal. That is precisely what God calls our turning away from him. The Hebrews thought that he would be satisfied with some religious rituals and rule keeping. God calls them an "adulterous" wife, of all things:

Long ago you broke off your yoke
    and tore off your bonds;
    you said, "I will not serve you!"
Indeed, on every high hill
    and under every spreading tree
    you lay down as a prostitute.

(Jer. 2:20 NIV)

But you trusted in your beauty and used your fame to become a prostitute. You lavished your favors on anyone who passed by and your beauty became his. (Ezek. 16:15 NIV)

The hero's heart has been broken. He rails with a jealous fury that flows only from a Lover who has been rejected:

> Because you have forgotten me
>   and trusted in false gods.
> I will pull up your skirts over your face
>   that your shame may be seen—
> your adulteries and lustful neighings,
>   your shameless prostitution!
>   (Jer. 13:25–27 NIV)

I will sentence you to the punishment of women who commit adultery and who shed blood; I will bring upon you the blood vengeance of my wrath and jealous anger. (Ezek. 16:38 NIV)

But the story does not finish with their divorce. True love never fails; it always perseveres. God will fight for his beloved. So the Old Testament ends with a promise of reconciliation:

> Therefore I will block her path with thornbushes;
>   I will wall her in so that she cannot find her way.
> She will chase after her lovers but not catch them;
>   she will look for them but not find them.
> Then she will say,
>   "I will go back to my husband as at first . . ."
> Therefore I am now going to allure her;
>   I will lead her into the desert
>   and speak tenderly to her . . .

> "In that day," declares the LORD,
>> "you will call me 'my husband';
>> you will no longer call me 'my master.'"
>>> (Hos. 2:6–7, 14, 16 NIV)

"That day" comes when Jesus appears on the scene and announces himself as the Bridegroom (Matt. 9:15). And when he says to us, "I am going there to prepare a place for you. And if I go and prepare a place for you, I will come back and take you to be with me that you also may be where I am," he is making his proposal (John 14:2–3 NIV). In the culture of the day, these are the very words a young man would say to his fiancée. Once the suitor secured the hand of his bride, he would return to his father's house and build the additional room that would be their bridal suite. (Couples moved into the home of the groom's parents.) It was "preparing a place for her." When all was ready, he would come for her and take her to be with him, so that where he is, she would also be.

We, the beloved, have become betrothed to the Bridegroom. John the Baptist said, "The bride belongs to the bridegroom. The friend who attends the bridegroom waits and listens for him, and is full of joy when he hears the bridegroom's voice" (John 3:29 NIV). We are in the time of waiting for the Bridegroom to return. By the end of the love story in Revelation 22 (vv. 17, 20 NIV), the church is practically panting for the return of Christ:

> The Spirit and the bride say, "Come!" And let him who hears say, "Come!" Whoever is thirsty, let him come; and whoever wishes, let him take the free gift of the water of life . . . He who testifies to these things says, "Yes, I am coming soon." Amen. Come, Lord Jesus.

Notice that it is the *bride* who is panting. How does a bride pant? As if for a lover who has long been away. She pants like the Beloved in Song of Songs: "Come, my lover, let us go to the countryside . . . There I will give you my love" (7:11–12 NIV). We are waiting for our Love to come. Augustine declared, "The whole life of the good Christian is a holy longing. What you desire ardently, as yet you do not see . . . By withholding of the vision, God extends the longing; through longing he extends the soul, by extending he makes room in it." So, said Augustine, "let us long because we are to be filled . . . that is our life, to be exercised by longing." And when the Bridegroom of our souls comes, what then? This engagement is headed toward a consummation.

THE CONSUMMATION OF THE AFFAIR
(What *Is* Worship, After All?)

The older Christian wedding vows contained these amazing words: "With my body, I thee worship." Maybe our forefathers weren't so prudish after all; maybe they understood sex far better than we do. To give yourself over to another, passionately and nakedly, to adore that person body, soul, and spirit—we know there is something special, even sacramental about sex. It requires trust and abandonment, guided by a wholehearted devotion. What else can this be but worship? After all, God employs explicitly sexual language to describe faithfulness (and unfaithfulness) to him. For us creatures of the flesh, sexual intimacy is the closest parallel we have to real worship. Even the world knows this. Why else would sexual ecstasy become the number one rival to communion with God? The best impostors succeed because they are nearly indistinguishable from what they are trying to imitate. We worship sex because we don't know how to worship God. But we will. Peter Kreeft writes,

This spiritual intercourse with God is the ecstasy hinted at in all earthly intercourse, physical or spiritual. It is the ultimate reason why sexual passion is so strong, so different from other passions, so heavy with suggestions of profound meanings that just elude our grasp. (*Everything You Wanted to Know About Heaven*)

Don't let your disappointing experiences cloud your understanding of this. We have grown cynical, as a society, about whether intimacy is really possible. To the degree that we have abandoned soul-oneness, we have sought out merely sex, physical sex, to ease the pain. But the full union is no longer there; the orgasm comes incomplete; its heart has been taken away. Many have been deeply hurt. Sometimes, we must learn from what we have not known, let it teach us what *ought* to be.

God's design was that the two shall become one flesh. The physical oneness was meant to be the expression of a total interweaving of being. Is it any wonder that we crave this? Our alienation is removed, if only for a moment, and in the paradox of love, we are at the same time known and taken beyond ourselves. In *The Mystery of Marriage* Mike Mason asserts,

For many people, certainly, sex is the most powerful and moving experience that life has to offer, and more overwhelmingly holy than anything that happens in church. For great masses of people, sex is the one force which can actually tip men and women completely off their accustomed centers of gravity and lift them, however briefly, right out of themselves.

As Allender says, our hearts live for "an experience of worship that fills our beings with a joy that is so deeply in awe of the other that we are barely aware of ourselves." Many people have a hard time conceiving of this kind of intimacy with God. For their entire lives they have related to him in a distant, though reverent way. Our worship services don't get anywhere near something like our wedding nights. Men in particular have a hard time relating to the bridal imagery used in Scripture. Do we take on femininity to relate to God? What does it mean to *know* God as our Lover?

THE BEAUTY AND STRENGTH OF GOD

It is a mystery almost too great to mention, but God is the expression of the very thing we seek in each other. For do we not bear God's image? Are we not a living portrait of God? Indeed we are, and in a most surprising place—in our *gender*. "So God created man in his own image, in the image of God he created him; male and female he created them" (Gen. 1:27 NIV). Follow me closely now. Gender—masculinity and femininity—is how we bear the image of God. "I thought that there was only one kind of soul," said a shocked friend. "And God sort of poured those souls into male or female bodies." Many people believe something like that. But it contradicts the Word of God. We bear his image as men and women, and God does not have a body. So it must be at the level of the soul—the eternal part of us—that we reflect God. The text is clear; it is *as a man* or *as a woman* that the image is bestowed.

God wanted to show the world something of his strength. Is he not a great warrior? Has he not performed the daring rescue of his beloved? And this is why he gave us the sculpture that is man. Men bear the image of God in their dangerous, yet inviting strength. Women, too, bear the image of God, but in a much different way. Is not God a being of great mystery and beauty? Is there not something tender and alluring about the essence of the Divine? And this is why he gave us the sculpture that is woman.

You men will know what Mason means, though perhaps you've never made the connection:

> My wife's body is brighter and more fascinating than a flower, shier than any animal, and more breathtaking than a thousand sunsets. To me her body is the most awesome thing in creation. Trying to look at her, just trying to take in her wild, glorious beauty . . . I catch a glimpse of what it means that men and women have been made in the image of God. If even the image is this dazzling, what must the Original be like? (*The Mystery of Marriage*)

What, indeed. God is the source of all masculine power; God is also the fountain of all feminine allure. Come to think of it, he is the wellspring of everything that has ever romanced your heart. The thundering strength of a waterfall, the delicacy of a flower, the stirring capacity of music, the richness of wine. The masculine and the feminine that fill all creation come from the same heart. What we have sought, what we have tasted in part with our earthly lovers, we will come face-to-face with in our True Love. For the incompleteness that we seek to relieve in the deep embrace of our earthly love is never fully healed. The union does not last, whatever the poets and pop artists may say. Morning comes and we've got to get out of bed and off to our day, incomplete once more. But oh, to have it healed forever; to drink deeply from that fount of which we've had only a sip; to dive into that sea in which we have only waded.

And so a man like Charles Wesley can pen these words: "Jesus, Lover of my soul, let me to thy bosom fly," while Catherine of Siena can pray, "O fire surpassing every fire because you alone are the fire that burns without consuming! . . . Yet your consuming does not distress the soul but fattens her with insatiable love."

The French mystic Madame Guyon can write, "I slept not all night, because Thy love, O my God, flowed in me like delicious oil, and burned as a fire . . . I love God far more than the most affectionate lover among men loves his earthly attachment." And at the same time a monk, St. John of the Cross, can say,

> I abandoned and forgot myself,
> laying my face on my Beloved;
> all things ceased; I went out from myself
> leaving my cares
> forgotten among the lilies.

Where else are we told about oil and lilies? In Song of Songs. Is there sex in heaven? It would be better to ask, Is there worship in heaven?

THE SHARED AFFAIR

"O, rejoice beyond a common joy, and set it down with gold on lasting pillars!" This is the cry sent up at the end of Shakespeare's play *The Tempest*. What is the reason for such uncommon rejoicing? That though treason, and foul play, and a shipwreck had for so long separated families, lovers, even kingdoms, they have all been reunited. In hope against hope, they have been restored to one another.

> In one voyage
> Did Claribel her husband find at Tunis,
> And Ferdinand, her brother, found a wife
> Where he himself was lost, Prospero his dukedom
> In a poor isle, and all of us ourselves
> When no man was his own.

It is a manifestation of the humility of God that he creates a kingdom so rich in love that he should not be our all, but that others should be precious to us as well. Even in Eden, before the Fall, while Adam walked in Paradise with his God, even then God said, "It is not good for the man to be alone" (Gen. 2:18 NIV). He gives to us the joy of community, of family and friends to share in the Sacred Romance.

Is it not the nature of true love—to be generous in love? This is something of the reason that married couples long to have children; they want others to share in their happiness. The embrace of lovers does not stay confined to the lovers; rather, it builds a home, it fills a household. And so our longing for intimacy reaches beyond our "one and only." We come to discover that others mean so very much to us. There is no joy like the joy of reunion because there is no sorrow like the sorrow of separation. To lose those we love and wonder if we shall ever see them again—this is our deepest grief.

In 1991, Eric Clapton lost his only son, five-year-old Connor. The little boy fell from a window of their Manhattan apartment, plunging forty-nine stories to his death. Clapton channeled his grief into writing the heart-wrenching song "Tears in Heaven." In it he puts words to one of our deepest questions,

> Would you know my name
> If I saw you in heaven?
> Would it be the same
> If I saw you in heaven?

Oh, how much hangs on the word *if*. Jesus wept at the funeral of his dear friend Lazarus. I'm not sure we understand his tears because we do not share his strange carelessness about death. He has told us again and again not to fear it. (At the approach of his own death, he tells his closest friends to be *glad*, for heaven's sake.) On reaching Lazarus's grieving sister Martha, Jesus makes the astounding statement that those who are his will simply "never die" (John 11:26 NIV). He then comes to the grave site and weeps. Certainly, the tears are not for Lazarus, for according to Jesus, Lazarus is quite well. Jesus weeps for Martha and Mary, and for all of us who suffer loss. I think he weeps not only for our loss, but also for our inability to see beyond it. Dare I say, sometimes our refusal to see beyond it?

I have tasted grief, drunk deeply from its bitter cup. It is the most awful experience in this life. Death truly is the enemy (1 Cor. 15:26). But much of our grief comes because we have not dislodged that *if* from our hearts. As Willard explains,

> Once we have grasped our situation in God's full world, the startling disregard Jesus and the New Testament writers had for "physical death" suddenly makes sense. Paul bluntly states . . . that Jesus abolished death—simply did away with it.
>
> To one group of his day, who believed that "physical death" was the cessation of the individual's existence, Jesus said, "God is not the God of the dead, but of the living" (Luke 20:38). His meaning was that those who love and are loved by God are not allowed to cease to exist, because they are God's treasures. He delights in them and intends to hold onto them. He has even prepared for them an individualized eternal work in his vast universe. (*The Divine Conspiracy*)

I'll say more about that work in the next chapter. What is vital for us to grasp now, Willard says, is simply this: "*The life we now have as the persons we now are will continue in the universe in which we now exist.*" By all means we shall know each other's name—not *if*—but *when* we see each other in God's great kingdom. We'll hold each other's hands, and far better than that. The naked intimacy, the real knowing that we enjoy with God, we shall enjoy with each other. George MacDonald wrote, "I think we shall be able to pass into and through each other's very souls as we please, knowing each other's thought and being, along with our own, and so being *like* God."

Brent used to call it multiple intimacy without promiscuity. It is what the ancients meant by the communion of saints. All of the joy that awaits us in the sea of God's love will be multiplied over and over as we share with each other in the Grand Affair. John Donne captures this beautifully:

> All mankind is of one author, and is one volume; when one man dies, one chapter is not torn out of the book, but translated into a better language; and every chapter must be so translated; God employs several translators: some pieces are translated by age, some by sickness, some by war, some by justice; but God's hand is in every translation; *and his hand shall bind up all our scattered leaves again*, for that library where every book shall lie open to one another.

Imagine the stories that we'll hear. And all the questions that shall finally have answers. "What were you thinking when you drove the old Ford out on the ice?" "Did you hear that Betty and Dan got back together? But of course you did—you were probably involved in that, weren't you?" "How come you never told us about your time in the war?" "Did you ever know how much I loved you?" And the answers won't be one-word answers, but story after story, a feast of wonder and laughter and glad tears.

The setting for this will be a great party, the wedding feast of the Lamb. Now, you've got to get images of Baptist receptions entirely out of your mind—folks milling around in the church gym, holding Styrofoam cups of punch, wondering what to do with themselves. You've got to picture an Italian wedding or, better, a Jewish wedding. They roll up the rugs and push back the furniture. There is *dancing*: "Then maidens will dance and be glad, young men and old as well" (Jer. 31:13 NIV). There is *feasting*: "On this mountain the LORD Almighty will prepare a feast of rich food for all peoples" (Isa. 25:6 NIV). (Can you imagine what kind of cook God must be?) And there is *drinking*—the feast God says he is preparing includes "a banquet of aged wine—the best of meats and the finest of wines." In fact, at his Last Supper our Bridegroom said he will not drink of "the fruit of the vine until the kingdom of God comes" (Luke 22:18 NIV). Then he'll pop a cork.

> And the people came together
> and the people came to dance
> and they danced like a wave upon the sea.

It was one of Brent's favorite lines from the poet Yeats. Stasi reminded me the other night of the last time Brent was in our home. For several years he and Ginny shared their lives with us and two other couples, all dear friends, in a covenant group. We'd meet twice a month or so, to talk about life. It was a place to know and be known, to come in out of the winds of the world and mend your sails. On this night, I'd asked everyone to bring a piece of art that he loved—a song, or a poem, or perhaps a film clip. Art is a glimpse into our hearts, and you can learn so much about someone when he shares with you something that has stirred his soul. Our conversation flowed from laughter to tears as we talked about each person's "window of the soul." The evening was winding to a close when Leigh offered to play the song she had brought. "It makes me think of heaven," she said, a little embarrassed. Heaven hadn't been part of the discussion 'til that moment. It was a joyful, upbeat, you've-got-to-get-up-and-dance kind of song, and soon we all were, swinging and jitter-bugging and just sort of hopping around the living room, none of us great dancers, but everyone celebrating the banquet to come. It was the last time we would all be together.

Until the Party begins.

CHAPTER NINE

THE
ADVENTURE BEGINS

And in the perfect time, O perfect God,
When we are in our home, our natal home,
When joy shall carry every sacred load,
And from its life and peace no heart shall roam,
What if thou make us able to make like thee—
To light with moons, to clothe with greenery,
To hang gold sunsets o'er a rose and purple sea!

—George MacDonald

Enter into the joy of your master.

—Jesus of Nazareth

We must explore one more aspect of our future if we are to recover heart for the journey of our lives. For though it will be unspeakable joy to live forever in a fully restored universe with the company of the truly intimate, it is not enough. There is something core to our being and set within our deepest desires that remains untouched. For as the nineteenth-century preacher Thomas Chalmers wrote, one of the "Grand Essentials" of human happiness is having something to *do*. I think the fear of being bored is an unspoken fear of many people about the life that is coming. After all, the never-ending sing-along in the sky isn't exactly breathtaking. Spending a weekend at the beach beats that hands down. Our lives in the coming kingdom will be surrounded with great beauty and our hearts filled with love, but what will we *do* with ourselves forever and ever? I have yet to meet a Christian who has more than the faintest notion of what his life will entail beyond the eternal church service. "I guess it will be good," sighed one friend. But guesses are not good enough in the journey of desire. We must *know*.

We've somehow overlooked a line in the parable of the talents, a single sentence that speaks volumes about the connection between our present and future life. As you'll recall, the landowner in the story has been away on a journey. In the parallel version told in Luke, the parable of the minas, he is a man of "noble birth" who has gone to "a distant country to have himself appointed king" (19:11–27 NIV). Upon his return, he rewards those faithful members of his staff in a way that at first seems, well, like no reward at all: "You have been faithful with a few things; I will put you in charge of many things." Luke's version has it this way: "Because you have been trustworthy in a very small manner, take charge of ten cities." This is their bonus— more to do? Wouldn't a vacation make a better reward? My boys clean their rooms so they can go out and play, not so they can clean the rest of the house. Yet Jesus thinks that he is sharing something delightful with us. The landowner then says, "Come and share your master's happiness." Or, as the King James has it, "Enter thou into the joy of thy lord" (Matt. 25:23). To understand what he means, we must have a closer look at God's joyful activity and our inherent design.

THE JOY OF THE MASTER

How marvelous it is to watch a master artist at work. We enjoyed a wonderful performance of Chausson's *Poeme for Violin and Orchestra* last night. The young woman who played the lead violin was simply beautiful in her long white gown, her graceful arms working the bow and strings with finesse. It was a joy just to watch her play. And the *Poeme* itself is an enchanting piece of music, almost ethereal. It fit her and the mood of the summer evening perfectly. And so it was with one accord that the audience rose in applause at the close of the performance.

Something similar happened at the opening of Genesis. As creation was unfolding from the hands of the Master, like wet clay on a potter's wheel, a great ovation erupted: "The morning stars sang together and all the angels shouted for joy" (Job 38:7 NIV). But of course. He has just finished sculpting the islands of Greece so that their white sandy beaches perfectly rim those azure seas. Then he watered the jungles of Malaysia to sustain an exotic array of orchids, after which he painted sunsets over the Sahara and hurled the Himalayas upward, treacherous peaks scraping the roof of the world.

And he doesn't stop there. Into this breathtaking setting of a thousand different habitats God places "the fish of the sea and the birds of the air and . . . every living creature that moves on the ground" (Gen. 1:28 NIV). Chameleons and caribou, porcupines and porpoises. How do we begin to describe this God whose image we bear? *Artistic* is the only word that even comes close. *Powerful, awesome, majestic*—yet *intricate, delicate, whimsical. Creative,* without a doubt. And that was just the beginning. Although God rested on the seventh day, he hasn't been lying around ever since.

Jesus said, "My Father is always at his work to this very day, and I, too, am working" (John 5:17 NIV). For many people this is a new thought—that God is still quite active. Life has led them to believe that he may have gotten things off to a great start, but then he left on vacation or perhaps went to attend to more important matters. But the creative overture recorded in Genesis was only the first movement of a great symphony that has been swelling ever since. The opening notes were not *staccato*, but *sostenuto*, ongoing, unfolding. He's not just sitting around on a throne somewhere. The psalmist proclaimed of God's work today,

He wraps himself in light as with a garment;
he stretches out the heavens like a tent
and lays the beams of his upper chambers on their waters.
He makes the clouds his chariot
and rides on the wings of the wind . . .
He makes springs pour water into the ravines;
it flows between the mountains.
They give water to all the beasts of the field;
the wild donkeys quench their thirst.
The birds of the air nest by the waters;
they sing among the branches.
He waters the mountains from his upper chambers;
the earth is satisfied by the fruit of his work.
He makes grass grow for the cattle,
and plants for man to cultivate–
bringing forth food from the earth:
wine that gladdens the heart of man,
oil to make his face shine,
and bread that sustains his heart.

(Ps. 104:2–3, 10–15 NIV)

The only way to describe his ongoing creative activity is *extravagant*. Thunderclouds gather over the prairies, and afterward he scatters wildflowers as far as the eye can see. He fills the oceans with orcas and urchins and who knows what. A single maple leaf is woven with greater intricacy than the finest French lace—even though it will fall with the winds of autumn. New stars are born every day; a new sunset painted and swept away each night. Such magnificent generosity. No composer ever gave so many free concerts. MacDonald had it right: "Gloriously wasteful, O my Lord, art thou!"

You don't suppose he experiences his part in running the universe as drudgery, do you? Did Margot Fonteyn and Rudolf Nureyev love to dance? Does Michael Jordan love to play basketball? So God loves his work. He isn't ashamed to call it all "very good." Like a Master Craftsman offering a glimpse into his workshop, he asks Job,

> Have you ever given orders to the morning,
>   or shown the dawn its place? . . .
> Have you journeyed to the springs of the sea
>   or walked in the recesses of the deep? . . .
> Have you entered the storehouses of the snow
>   or seen the storehouses of the hail? . . .
> Can you bind the beautiful Pleiades?
>   Can you loose the cords of Orion?
> Can you bring forth the constellations in their seasons
>   or lead out the Bear with its cubs? . . .
> Do you send the lightning bolts on their way?
>   Do they report to you, "Here we are"? . . .
> Do you hunt the prey for the lioness
>   and satisfy the hunger of the lions? . . .
> Do you give the horse his strength
>   or clothe his neck with a flowing mane?
>   (Job 38:12–40; 39:19 NIV)

On and on he goes with a pride that befits his grandeur. You see, Job has come to the point where he wonders, rather loudly, whether God is "on the job" anymore. This is God's answer, and it goes on for two more chapters. The frost each morning? That's mine. The ostrich and hippo—mine too. I'm watching over the young doe when she gives birth; the eagle soars at my command. A jealous indignation characterizes these words, the sort of emotion that is aroused when someone criticizes our most cherished work. You see, it is God's *delight* to do all these things. Dallas Willard notes,

> We should, to begin with, think that God leads a very interesting life, and that he is full of joy. Undoubtedly he is the most joyous being in the universe. The abundance of his love and generosity is inseparable from his infinite joy. All of the good and beautiful things from which we occasionally drink tiny droplets of soul-exhilarating joy, God continuously experiences in all their breadth and depth . . . We are enraptured by a well-done movie sequence or by a few bars from an opera or lines from a poem. We treasure our great experiences for a lifetime, and we may have very few of them. But he is simply one great inexhaustible and eternal experience of all that is good and true and beautiful and right. This is what we must think of when we hear theologians and philosophers speak of him as a perfect being. *This is his life.* (*The Divine Conspiracy*)

And it is *this* life, with all its joyful creativity and power and unending happiness, that he says he is going to share with us. This is "the joy of your master" that we are to be welcomed into. It rather beats harps and halos, wouldn't you say? For we long to find our place in the world, caring for and developing creation in all its diverse potential. It is this for which we were made.

LITTLE GODS

"So God created man in his own image, in the image of God he created him; male and female he created them." Thus is humanity trumpeted onto the scene in verse 27 of the first chapter of Genesis (NIV). It is a passage familiar to most of us. Too familiar perhaps, for we rarely wonder about what it means. Right here, at the beginning of our existence, is the single phrase our Creator uses to characterize us, and most of us haven't the foggiest idea what it implies. If we were reading the Scripture for the story it is (and not like an encyclopedia, as many do), we would have in mind all that has transpired up to this moment. We have been watching the God whose image we bear. What do we know about him at this point? What has he been up to? Creating the heavens and the earth. Islands and caribou and wildflowers. This is what he has been doing. *This is all we know of God* when we reach the point at which we are compared to him.

If you were meeting a young man for the first time, and he was introduced to you as the "son of Einstein," you'd probably expect him to be rather bright. If you met a young woman as the "daughter of Nadia Comaneci," the Russian gymnast, you might assume she could turn a decent cartwheel. We expect greatness from the offspring of the great. To be introduced as the image bearers of God is full of anticipation. It would be as though we were introduced as the sons of a renowned artist, perhaps a Monet, or as the daughters of a graceful dancer, such as Martha Graham. It leads us to what to expect next. Jesus said, "Is it not written in your Law, 'I have said you are gods'?" (John 10:34 NIV). Why is it, then, that creativity rarely comes to mind when we think of how we reflect God? More often than not we think of godliness in moral terms. When we hear that so-and-so is a "godly person," we assume that he is devout, or perhaps self-sacrificing, and certainly more virtuous than most. But when Genesis declares we are God's image, it is describing not certain qualities of our character but *capacities of our nature*. This is why, when the essence of our likeness to God is announced, it is in the context of our *position* upon the earth, our place in creation:

> Then God said, "Let us make man in our image, in our likeness, *and let them rule* over the fish of the sea and the birds of the air, over the livestock, over all the earth, and over all the creatures that move along the ground." (Gen. 1:26 NIV, emphasis added)

In other words, we are *made* like God in our creative powers because we are to *be* like God in ruling the earth. The image implies a capacity, and the capacity assumes the creative legacy we shall carry on. "Those two phrases—'Let us make man in our Image,' and 'Let them rule'—must be taken together," says Ben Patterson. "Each modifies the other. To be like God is to rule the earth as he does. To rule the earth as he does is to be like God." Our original design was for a life of creative rule, to share in the overall care and development of God's creation. The poet writes because she is made in God's image; the builder loves to build for the same reason. Entrepreneurs risk capital ventures, baseball players go to the batting cages, and cooks experiment with spices all for the same reason. It is what we *are*.

ON MOZART AND MARTHA STEWART

"Somehow," notes Os Guinness, "we human beings are never happier than when we are expressing the deepest gifts that are truly us." Now, some children are gifted toward science, and others are born athletes. But whatever their specialty, *all* children are inherently creative. Give them a barrel of Legos and a free afternoon and my boys will produce an endless variety of spaceships and fortresses and who knows what. It comes naturally to children; it's in their *nature*, their design as little image bearers. Set a group of kindergartners down with sheets of paper and tubs of finger paint, and you don't have to provide directions. They know what to do. In fact, paint and paper aren't even necessary; chocolate pudding and a nearby wall will do nicely. A pack of boys let loose in a wood soon becomes a major Civil War reenactment. A chorus of girls, upon discovering a trunk of skirts and dresses, will burst into the *Nutcracker Suite*. The right opportunity reveals the creative nature.

This is precisely what happens when God shares with mankind his own artistic capacity and then sets us down in a paradise of unlimited potential. It is an act of creative *invitation*, like providing Monet with a studio for the summer, stocked full of brushes and oils and empty canvases. Or like giving Mozart full use of an orchestra and a concert hall for an autumn of composing. Or like setting Martha Stewart loose in a gourmet kitchen on a snowy winter weekend, just before the holidays. You needn't provide instructions or motivation; all you have to do is release them to be who they are, and remarkable things will result. As the poet Hopkins wrote, "What I do is me: for that I came."

Oh, how we long for this—for a great endeavor that draws upon our every faculty, a great "life's work" that we could throw ourselves into. "I was made for this," said one friend who after years of hesitation finally pursued his dream of becoming a high school teacher. "It energizes me." "After years in a wasteland," moaned another, "all I want is to be released to be who I am." His career had not panned out, and as he saw his most productive days slipping by, he longed to find his place. "God has created us and our gifts for a place of his choosing," says Guinness, "and we will only be ourselves when we are finally there." Our creative nature is essential to who we are as human beings—as image bearers—and it brings us great joy to live it out with freedom and skill. Even if it's a simple act such as working on your photo albums or puttering in the garden—these, too, are how we have a taste of what was meant to rule over a small part of God's great kingdom. Willard points out:

> Here is a truth that reaches into the deepest part of what it means to be a person . . . that we are made to "have dominion" within an appropriate domain of reality. This is the core of the likeness or image of God in us and is the basis of the destiny for which we were formed. We are, all of us, never-ceasing spiritual beings with a unique eternal calling to count for good in God's great universe . . . In creating human beings God made them to rule, to reign, to have dominion in a limited sphere. Only so can they be persons. (*The Divine Conspiracy*)

THE MISERIES OF A DETHRONED MONARCH

During a long layover at O'Hare, I studied the man who sells popcorn from a little stand in one of the terminal hallways. He sat silently on a stool as thousands of people rushed by. Occasionally, every fifteen minutes or so, someone would stop and buy a bag. He would scoop the popcorn from the bin, take the money, and make change—all without a word being spoken between them. When the brief encounter was over, he would resume his place on the stool, staring blankly, his shoulders hunched over. I wondered at his age; he seemed well past fifty. How long had that been his profession? Could he possibly make a living at it? His face wore a weary expression of resignation tinged with shame. *Adam*, I thought, *what happened?* Did he know how far his situation was from his true design? Somehow he knew, even if he didn't know the Story. His sadness was testimony to it. I thought of Pascal, that all our miseries prove our greatness: "They are the miseries of a dethroned monarch."

Some people love what they do. They are the fortunate souls, who have found a way to link what they are truly gifted at (and therefore what brings them joy) with a means of paying the bills. But most of the world merely toils to survive, and no one gets to use his gifts all the time. On top of that, there is the curse of thorns and thistles, the futility that tinges all human efforts at the moment. As a result, we've come to think of work as a result of the Fall. You can see our cynicism in the fact that we've chosen the cartoon character Dilbert as the icon of our working days. His is a hopeless life of futility and anonymity in the bowels of a large corporation. We don't even know what he does—only that it's meaningless. We identify with him, feeling at some deep level the apparent futility of our lives. Even if we are loved, it is not enough. We yearn to be *fruitful*, to do something of meaning and value that flows naturally out of the gifts and capacities of our souls. But of course—we were meant to be the kings and queens of the earth.

Dorothy Sayers once wrote, "Work is not, primarily, a thing one does to live, but the thing one lives to do." If only it were so; if only we could land our "dream job," where we'd be paid to do what we love. Some actually go out and do it. A friend took off several years ago to be a hunting and fishing guide in Alaska. He's having a ball. Another friend had a chance to work on Broadway; his wife said to me afterward, "John was made for this. All the experiences of his life had led up to this very thing." The rest of us look on from the sidelines with longing, held back from our dreams by fear or heartache or the demands of the life we do have. No wonder we hear the rewards in the parable with such disappointed ears—it sounds as though we'll lose even those few hours of private joy we manage to squeeze in on the weekend and take on some sort of eternal task. But what if it were the opposite? What if the master's invitation was to do, like Hopkins, what is *you*? What if you were given the *freedom* (the permission) and the *power* (all the resources necessary) to do exactly what you were always meant to do?

THE MONARCHY RESTORED

Let's come back for a moment to the restoration of the earth. In Romans 8 (NIV), Paul says something outrageous. He says that all our sufferings are "not worth comparing" with the glory that will be revealed in us. It seems hard to believe, given the way life can break your heart. The human race has seen an unspeakable amount of suffering. What can possibly make that seem like nothing? "The glory that will be revealed in us" (8:18). The Great Restoration. Paul then goes on to say, "The creation waits in eager expectation for the sons of God to be revealed" (8:19). The release of a fully restored creation is being more or less held back, waiting upon *our* restoration. Why? Because only then can we handle it. Only when we ourselves have been restored can we take our place again as the kings and queens of creation. Or did you not know? The day is coming when Christ will appoint you as one of his regents over his great and beautiful universe. This has been his plan all along.

> When the Son of Man comes in his glory, and all the angels with him, he will sit on his throne in heavenly glory. All the nations will be gathered before him, and he will separate the people one from another as a shepherd separates the sheep from the goats. He will put the sheep on his right and the goats on his left.

Then the King will say to those on his right, "Come, you who are blessed by my Father; take your inheritance, *the kingdom prepared for you since the creation of the world."* (Matt. 25:31–34 NIV, emphasis added)

Who then is the faithful and wise servant, whom the master has put in charge of the servants in his household to give them their food at the proper time? It will be good for that servant whose master finds him doing so when he returns. I tell you the truth, *he will put him in charge of all his possessions.* (Matt. 24:45–47 NIV, emphasis added)

And they will *reign* for ever and ever. (Rev. 22:5 NIV, emphasis added)

Think for a moment. The One who created you and set all those loves and gifts in your heart, the One who has shaped all your life experiences (including the ones that seem to make no sense), this God has prepared a place for you that is a more than perfect fit for all your gifts and quirks and personality traits— even those you don't know you have. Christ is not joking when he says that we shall inherit the kingdom prepared for us and shall reign with him forever. We will take the position for which we have been uniquely made and will rule *as he does*—meaning with creativity and power.

I think back upon God's questions to Job: "Have you ever given orders to the morning? Do you hunt the prey for the lioness?" And like a young apprentice in the presence of a master, something in my heart says cautiously (yet eagerly), "No . . . but I'd like to!" And so Willard writes,

We will not sit around looking at one another or at God for eternity but will join the eternal Logos, "reign with him," in the endlessly ongoing creative work of God. It is for this that we were each individually intended, as both kings and priests (Exod. 19:6; Rev. 5:10) . . . A place in God's creative order has been reserved for each one of us from before the beginnings of cosmic existence. His plan is for us to develop, as apprentices to Jesus, to the point where we can take our place in the ongoing creativity of the universe. (*The Divine Conspiracy*)

Much of the activity of God in our lives is bringing us to the place where he can entrust us with this kind of influence. God takes our training so seriously because he fully intends to promote us. Will it be joy? Does Stephen Hawking enjoy physics? Does Mark McGwire enjoy hitting it out of the park? There are so many ways this "reigning" will be expressed—as unique and varied as there are human souls. God has quite a few "possessions," and it's going to take a lot of looking after by men and women uniquely fitted for the task.

I am not a scientist; but I am told by those who are of the great adventure in exploring the beauty revealed in the structures of physics or molecular biology. I don't go in for organizational structures and master planning, but I have friends who can talk about them for hours. To each his own—literally. Each person will live out the passion of his heart, set there by the Creator from before the beginning of time. I should like one day to paint with the grace of Monet, or plumb the wonders of physics with Einstein. Perhaps I shall. There is work enough to be done.

THE GLORIOUS FREEDOM

"Life," as a popular saying goes, "is not a dress rehearsal. Live it to the fullest." What a setup for a loss of heart. No one gets all he desires; no one even comes close. If this is it, we are lost. But what if life *is* a dress rehearsal? What if the real production is about to begin? That is precisely what Jesus says; he tells us that we are being shaped, prepared, groomed for a part in the grand drama that is coming. In *The Call*, Guinness writes about a delightful story told by Artie Shaw, a famous clarinetist during the big band era:

> Maybe twice in my life I reached what I wanted to. Once we were playing "These Foolish Things" and at the end the band stops and I play a little cadenza. That cadenza—no one can do it better. Let's say it's five bars. That's a very good thing to have done in a lifetime. An artist should be judged by his best, just as an athlete. Pick out my one or two best things and say, "That's what we did: all the rest was rehearsal."

All the rest was rehearsal—not for just a few shining moments, but for an eternity of joy. Realizing this is immensely freeing. How many of your plans take an unending future into account? "Let's see, I'm going to be alive forevermore, so . . . if I don't get this done now, I'll get to it later." This is so important, for no human life reaches its potential here.

I was talking with a playwright several years ago. His career was not panning out the way he deeply wanted it to, and he was becoming rather depressed. It wasn't a matter of being unqualified; he was, and is, a very gifted writer. But few playwrights achieve anything like success. Life wasn't inviting him to be who he was—yet. He had never once considered that he would be a great writer in the coming kingdom, and that he was merely in training now. His day was yet to come. Understanding that put his life in an entirely new light.

In Revelation 21, John describes the New Jerusalem, the city of God come to earth. It is a place of exquisite beauty and grandeur. And then he adds an odd statement: "The kings of the earth will bring *their* splendor into it" (v. 24 NIV, emphasis added). It seems hard to believe that we could add anything to the splendor God creates, but that is exactly what we are designed for and what our future involves. How amazing it will be to have our souls released into their true destiny, in a world no longer stained by sin or under the curse. To throw ourselves into some wonderful enterprise, unhindered by our own weaknesses or the frustrations typical of a broken world. Gardeners dream of a spot of ground with rich soil and not a weed or sow bug to be found. They shall have it. Architects dream of the day they shall build their own designs and not merely carry out the plans of another. They shall. Like children eager to show off our precious creations, we shall bring them to our Father in Jerusalem, for glory and praise.

The Grand Affair heals the curse of isolation. The Great Adventure heals the curse of futility. The "glorious freedom" of the children of God is the freedom of being all we were meant to be. We won't be held back by anything anymore; no, we will finally hit our stride. We all know the frustration of failure, of missing the mark—getting the equation wrong, hitting the ball into the rough, misdiagnosing the patient. And most of us at one time or another have tasted the joy of getting it right. Not only will we find our place, but we will be empowered to do the very things we aim to do, with and for God. As C. S. Lewis wrote,

> The miracles that have already happened are, of course, as the Scripture often says, the first fruits of that cosmic summer which is presently coming on. Christ has risen, and so we shall rise. St. Peter for a few seconds walked on the water; and the day will come when there will be a remade universe, infinitely obedient to the will of glorified and obedient men, when we can do all things, when we shall be those gods that we are described as being in Scripture. (*The Grand Miracle*)

Three weeks after the wind ceased to blow, the sea lion had a dream. Now, as I told you before, there were other nights in which he had dreamed of the sea. But those were long ago and nearly forgotten. Even still, the ocean that filled his dreams this night was so beautiful and clear, so vast and deep, it was as if he were seeing it for the very first time. The sunlight glittered on its surface, and as he dived, the waters all around him shone like an emerald. If he swam quite deep, it turned to jade, cool and dark and mysterious. But he was never frightened, not at all. For I must tell you that in all his dreams of the sea, he had never before found himself in the company of other sea lions. This night there were many, round about him, diving and turning, spinning and twirling. They were playing.

Oh, how he hated to wake from that wonderful dream. The tears running down his face were the first wet thing he had felt in three weeks. But he did not pause even to wipe them away; he did not pause, in fact, for anything at all. He set his face to the east, and he began to walk as best a sea lion can.

"Where are you going?" asked the tortoise.

"I am going to find the sea."

CHAPTER TEN

ENTERING MORE DEEPLY INTO DESIRE

Blessed are those who hunger and thirst.
—Jesus of Nazareth

And in me wake hope, fear, boundless desire.
—George MacDonald

The devil sleepeth not, neither is the flesh as yet dead; there-
fore cease not to prepare thyself for the battle; for on thy
right hand and on thy left are enemies who never rest.
—Thomas à Kempis

I hope by now you see why I have spent three chapters trying to bring eternity out of the clouds and into our conscious lives. The dilemma of desire is the deepest dilemma we will ever face. Its dangers are deep and potentially fatal. How, then, shall we not lose heart? If we manage to somehow hang on to our desire, how do we keep from being consumed by it? The secret is known to all of us, though we may have forgotten that we know it. Who wants to fill up with snacks on Thanksgiving Day? Who goes out to buy presents for himself on Christmas Eve? Is there anyone in his right mind who looked for someone to date at his wedding rehearsal? When we are convinced that something delicious is about to be ours, we are free to live in expectation, and it draws us on in anticipation. There are three things that we must come to terms with in our deep heart. First, we must have life. Second, we cannot arrange for it. Third, it is coming. Now we are ready to proceed on our way.

BATTLE AND JOURNEY

Life is now a battle and a journey. As Eugene Peterson reminds us, "We must fight the forces that oppose our becoming whole; we must find our way through difficult and unfamiliar territory to our true home." It's not that there aren't joy and beauty, love and adventure now—there are. The invasion of the kingdom has begun. But life in its fullness has yet to come. So we must take seriously the care of our hearts. We must watch over our desire with a fierce love and vigilance, as if we were protecting our most precious possession. We must do battle with the enemies of our hearts—those sirens that would seduce and shipwreck our desire and those arrows that aim to kill it outright. And we must journey forward, toward God, toward the Great Restoration and the Adventures to come. How awful to reach the end of life's road and find we haven't brought our hearts along with us.

So let me say it again: life is now a battle and a journey. This is the truest explanation for what is going on, the only way to rightly understand our experience. Life is not a game of striving and indulgence. It is not a long march of duty and obligation. It is not, as Henry Ford once said, "one damn thing after another." Life is a desperate quest through dangerous country to a destination that is, beyond all our wildest hopes, indescribably good. Only by conceiving of our days in this manner can we find our way safely through. You see, different roads lead different places. To find the Land of Desire, you must take the journey of desire.

You can't get there by any other means. If we are to take up the trail and get on with our quest, we've got to get our hearts back, which means getting our desire back.

RECOVERING DESIRE

I continue to be stunned by the level of deadness that most people consider normal and seem to be contented to live with. It had been more than a year since Diane and Ted first came to see me for counseling. As with most marriages, the real issues lay buried under years of just getting by, hidden beneath the way we've learned to live with each other so as not to rock the boat. Sadly, this way involves killing large regions of our hearts. And so their struggle toward intimacy required a lot of pain and hard work. But they stuck with it until they began to taste the true life of a real marriage. At this point Diane asked Ted about his deepest desires: "If I could be more of what you wanted in a woman, what do you secretly wish I would offer you?" It's a question that most men are dying to be asked. His response? Clean socks. That's all he could come up with. Life would be better, his marriage would be richer, if Diane would keep his drawer filled with clean socks. I wanted to throw him out the window.

I wasn't angry with Ted because his answer was unbelievably shallow or because it mocked all that his wife was seeking to offer him. I was angry because *it's just not true*. We are made in the image of God; we carry within us the desire for our true life of intimacy and adventure. To say we want less than that is to lie. Ted may believe that clean socks would satisfy him, but he is deceived. His satisfaction comes at the price of his soul.

When I brought up this very issue with a colleague, he sort of dismissed it all with the comment, "Not everyone longs like you do." I had to admit that much. But we were *meant* to. I thought of

The Weight of Glory, where Lewis says that "when we consider the unblushing promises of reward and the staggering nature of the rewards promised in the Gospels, it would seem that our Lord finds our desires not too strong, but too weak." My point precisely. Lewis is right:

> We are half-hearted creatures, fooling about with drink and sex and ambition, when infinite joy is offered us, like an ignorant child who wants to go on making mud pies in a slum because he cannot imagine what is meant by the offer of a holiday at the sea. We are far too easily pleased.

If only it were as strong as drink and sex and ambition. We've been bought off by clean socks and television. We'll sell our birthright for a little bit of pleasure and some peace and quiet. I understand. It hasn't taken us long to realize that life is not going to offer what we truly want, and so we've learned to reduce our desires to a more manageable size. But let's be honest about what we've done, and call it what it is: sin. The first step in the journey of desire is to stop pretending that we'd be happy with our equivalent of clean socks. Simone Weil said, "The danger is that the soul should persuade itself that it is not hungry." Recovering our true heart's desire may involve facing some very deep disappointment. Undoubtedly, it will require painful self-examination. But we do not need to fear what we will find, for our heart is our ally in this journey.

OUR DEEPEST HEART

Many committed Christians are wary about getting in touch with their desires, not because they want to settle for less, but because they fear that they will discover some dark hunger lurking in their hearts. As I've said, the father of lies takes many people out of the battle and ends their journey by keeping them in the shallows of their desire, tossing them a bone of pleasure, and thus convincing them that they are satisfied. However, once we begin to move from that place, his strategy changes. He threatens us from going into the deep waters by telling us that our core desires are evil. You might recall the scene in *Pilgrim's Progress* that takes place as Christian is making his way along the dark and dangerous trail through the Valley of the Shadow of Death:

> One thing I would not let slip; I took notice that now poor Christian was so confounded that he did not know his own voice; and thus I perceived it. One of the wicked ones got behind him, and stepped up softly to him, and whisperingly suggested many grievous blasphemies to him, which he verily thought had proceeded from his own mind. This put Christian more to it than anything that he met with before, even to think that he should now blaspheme him that he loved so much before; yet if he could have helped it, he would not have done it; but he had not the discretion either to stop his ears, or to know from whence these [thoughts] came.

The crisis for Christian is that he did not know his own voice, his true voice. He was convinced that the whispers of the enemy were his own desires. Far too many Christians today make the same dangerous assumption—that every thought and desire they experience is their own. "I could just lose myself at work." David was angry and resentful as he said this. He is struggling deeply in his marriage just now. "And no one would know the difference. I would still look married." "You are not a coward," I said. "I know you . . . that is not your heart. That is not the man you really want to be."

Listen to the promise of God to us in the new covenant: "I will give you a new heart and put a new spirit in you; I will remove from you your heart of stone and give you a heart of flesh" (Ezek. 36:26 NIV). For those who have been born of the Spirit and become new creatures in Christ, sin is no longer the truest thing about us. Since the coming of Christ, everything has changed. The joy of the new covenant is the transformation of our deepest being. As Christians, we have a new heart, and that means nothing less than this: our core desires are good. "I will put my law in their minds and write it on their hearts" (Jer. 31:33 NIV). We don't need to fear recovering our desire because our desire is from God and for God. That is what is most true about us. After several silent moments David said, "You're right. This is not what I most deeply want."

Yes, we still struggle with sin, with our tendency to kill desire or give our hearts over to false desires. But that is not who and what we truly are. If we really believe the new covenant, we'll be able to embrace our desire. So, let's come back to the simple question Jesus asks of us all: What do you want? Don't minimize it; don't try to make sure it sounds spiritual; don't worry about whether or not you can obtain it. Just stay with the question until you begin to get an answer. This is the way we keep current with our hearts.

WHAT DO YOU WANT?

"It's hard to be holy and passionate." Cindy sighed as she said this. A bright young woman and a sincerely committed follower of Christ, she's also a bit more vulnerable to men than she'd like to be. It seems that the only way Cindy can keep from chasing after physical intimacy with a man is to bury herself in grad school. But as I've said earlier, the "run from desire" approach never works, and she soon finds herself leaving the books for another compromis-

ing situation. "Why can't I get beyond this?" she asked. "I'm praying and reading my Bible every day. But still I fall." "What are you
looking for?" I asked in return. We sat in silence for a few minutes.
"I really don't know." "That's your problem . . . you don't know.
And so your unexamined desires rule you." After a few moments
she asked, "Is it pleasure? Excitement?" She was clueless. As intelligent as Cindy is, I wasn't surprised that she had no clue about
why she couldn't break her addiction to men. As a rule, most of us
live far from our hearts. We need to be much more acquainted
with them. We need to know what we want.

The path to a clearer knowledge of our desire depends on
how we've been handling it. Those who have buried desire
beneath years of duty and obligation may need to give all that a
rest so that their hearts can come to the surface. Abandon all but
the most essential duties for a while. You still have to pay the
bills, but everything you can jettison, you should. Do nothing
unless it reflects your true desire. Remember the Pharisees—
their religious activities deadened them to the point that they
couldn't even recognize God when he stood before them. When
our deepest treasure becomes our most dutiful burden, it really
kills our hearts. You might even need to give up going to church
for a while or reading your Bible. I stopped going to church for
a year; it was one of the most refreshing years of my life. I hadn't
abandoned God, and I very much sought out the company of my
spiritual companions. What I gave up was the performance of
having to show up every Sunday morning with my happy face
on. I suggested something similar to a young woman who had
really lost the joy of her faith. A few weeks later she wrote to me,
"I actually had a desire to read the Bible and pray without its
being a set time or a guilt trip! That's never happened before!"

Those who have been living to indulge desire will need to
give that a rest too. What does your heart feel when I suggest you

give up your obsession? Listen to the panic—there's something beneath it, something you need to know. Now, I understand that going cold turkey may seem overwhelming, unattainable. You may have tried that before and failed. Let me offer a more gentle approach. Simply stay in your desire for fifteen minutes longer than you usually do. When you're feeling a pull to the refrigerator or the gym or the bedroom, stop and let the desire just be; let it become more acute. Don't do anything with it. Let yourself feel it, and as you do, let your heart put some honest words to what you're feeling. You might be surprised what you find there.

I was walking down the hall at work one day, lost in my thoughts. Walking ahead of me, the same direction I was going, was a beautiful woman. I looked up and my heart said, *Wow!* Fearing that the beast of lust was rearing its ugly head, I tried to kill my reaction. It never works, and I knew it, so I decided instead to find out what was going on beneath what seemed to be an inappropriate response. Still walking along, with this beauty still in view, I asked my heart, *What do you mean by "wow"?* The next sentence literally popped out, unscripted, from someplace deep inside me: *The grand prize if you are truly a man.* I was stunned. I have lived that lie for a long time. How many young boys in our culture, just as they are entering adolescence, are introduced to sexuality as masculinity? Look at every ad designed for men. Whether it's for cars or sporting gear, clothes or beer, a beautiful siren is almost always posing seductively alongside. The message is beaten into us: if you're a man, you'll win the woman. I saw how long I had been haunted by that idea, and I also saw that what I was desiring was not an affair, but a truer sense of my masculinity.

This is something more than cognitive therapy, more than telling yourself the truth. It involves the hidden places of your heart, which are almost always revealed in your desire. But few of us take the time to look at the desire *beneath* the desire. A friend just spent thousands of dollars to undo a previous operation that tied her fallopian tubes. She wants to have another baby; no, she *needs* to have another baby. It has nothing to do with a baby. This is where she experiences being needed and wanted and loved. How many women derive their sense of self from their children? On and on it goes. Do we purchase a new home merely for more space, or does it mean security to us? We seek a better job. Might we be seeking a sense of identity, of being a successful person? It's not that the longing roused by any of these things is wrong. It's that we must learn what is actually *being* roused. The more attuned we are to our true desire, the less prone we'll be to impostors.

TEMPTATION

Then Jesus was led by the Spirit into the desert to be tempted by the devil. After fasting forty days and forty nights, he was hungry. The tempter came to him and said, "If you are the Son of God, tell these stones to become bread." Jesus answered, "It is written: 'Man does not live on bread alone, but on every word that comes from the mouth of God.'" (Matt. 4:1–4 NIV)

We can learn many things about the journey of desire in the story of Jesus' wilderness trial. First, "he was hungry." I am so grateful for that phrase. It helps me to believe in the humanity of Jesus. He didn't just glide along through life, untouched by the dilemma of desire. Because his hunger is real, we can learn something about ours. May says, "If we think of Jesus as truly human, as a real man who was truly vulnerable to attachment, then the way he responded to Satan's temptation reveals some things that are critically important." The first thing we learn is that we're going to hunger. It's normal; expect it. Jesus' hunger validates my own. I needn't be embarrassed by it, try to hide it, or diminish it in some way. Sometimes we feel guilty about the depth of our desire, and we end up repenting of the wrong thing.

The devil sees his opportune moment. He comes to Jesus as he comes to us—in our hunger. And what he says is simply this: "You don't have to stay hungry, you know. There are options." He's not lying at this point; there usually are options. There is often something we can do about our hunger, and the options increase the more we are willing to turn away from trusting God. The lie is that the options will bring us what we most deeply want and need. They won't. Every idol is an impostor. Jesus responds, "Those options are not true life." This is the first crucial moment—facing what the options really amount to and realizing "that's not really life." A deep, robust thirst—like we feel after a long, hot hike—can be quenched only by water. To be offered a hot fudge sundae wouldn't tempt us at all. And so we see the importance of entering into desire, of knowing full well what we're craving.

I look at what my friends eat—not one-tenth of it is real food. It is all impostors—canned this, microwaved that. Bread without any nutritional value; fruit juice that boasts "10 percent real juice." Thus they slowly starve themselves while feeling full. When we are out of shape, when we are in the habit of eating poorly, truly nourishing foods don't appeal to us. Better something rich, high in fat. Those mock our need while they appease our taste. But when we are fit, when we've been working out or just working hard in the field, we know what we want. Who would trade a hearty farmhouse dinner for a plate of marshmallows? The truly healthy desire knows what it wants. Had we desired more deeply, more clearly, we would have seen the offer for what it was. Knowing full well what our heart's real thirst was, we would have looked the impostor in the face and laughed. As Jesus did.

Then the devil took him to the holy city and had him stand on the highest point of the temple. "If you are the Son of God," he said, "throw yourself down. For it is written: 'He will command his angels concerning you, and they will lift you up in their hands, so that you will not strike your foot against a stone.'" Jesus answered him, "It is also written: 'Do not put the Lord your God to the test.'" (Matt. 4:5–7 NIV)

The second trial comes after we determine not to take matters into our own hands. By refusing to turn stones to bread, Jesus chooses to trust God. That is what we are saying when we refuse our options as well. Satan's reply is, "Oh, so you're going to trust your God. Fine. Prove he cares for you." He comes with an attack on God's heart toward us. This is almost inevitable for the thirsty soul. After we have chosen to remain in our thirst for a while, the doubts begin to creep in. *God, I know you love me. But I didn't expect I'd have to wait so long for what I desire.* We begin to wonder, *Do you care for me, God?* Satan jumps all over this, throwing fuel on the fire of our doubts. Jesus' response is our only hope: "I don't need to prove that God cares for me. He cares for me *now*." There is no other place to stand. As Allender says,

> If God's goodness is looked for primarily in turns of fortune . . . then the verdict on his heart towards us will always be pending on a new set of facts. We will, then, become either a judge ("How can God be good, if he let my son die?!") or a bargainer ("God, I'll know you are good if you bring my husband back to me"). God does not seem to show his goodness to those who peer through the lens of a skeptical examiner or a demanding negotiator. The Evil One uses the pain and confusion of a fallen world to shadow doubt over God's goodness. (*Bold Love*)

Jesus came to answer once and for all our question, "Do you care for me, God?" That is why the ground before the cross is the only place we can take a firm stand against the doubts that come in the journey of desire. We don't need for God to prove his love for us; he has, at the cross.

> Again, the devil took him to a very high mountain and showed him all the kingdoms of the world and their splendor. "All this I will give you," he said, "if you will bow down and worship me." Jesus said to him, "Away from me, Satan! For it is written: 'Worship the Lord your God, and serve him only.'" Then the devil left him, and angels came and attended him. (Matt. 4:8–11 NIV)

The cat's out of the bag. Satan has revealed his true aim. "You don't have to take the route of suffering," he says. "There are shortcuts. Just give your heart away." It all comes down to worship. What will we give our hearts away to, in return for the promise of life? May says this is "the ultimate invitation to idolatry." Jesus shuts Satan down: "There are no shortcuts, and my heart belongs to God alone."

Once we realize what a precious thing this is, the heart's desire, we must see that to guard it is worth our all. To neglect it is foolishness. To kill it is suicide. To allow it to wander aimlessly, to be trapped by the seductions of the evil one, is disaster. We must be *serious* about our happiness. And so Thomas à Kempis urges,

> The greatest, and indeed the whole impediment, is that we are not disentangled from our passions and lusts, neither do we endeavor to enter into that path of perfection which the saints have walked before us; and when any small adversity befalleth us, we are too quickly dejected, and turn ourselves to human comforts. If we would endeavor, like men of courage, to stand in the battle, surely we would feel the favorable assistance of God

from heaven. For he who giveth us occasion to fight, to the end that we may get the victory, is ready to succor those that fight manfully, and do trust in his grace. *(The Imitation of Christ)*

TUNING THE INSTRUMENT

So I tell you this, and insist on it in the Lord, that you must no longer live as the Gentiles do, in the futility of their thinking. They are darkened in their understanding and separated from the life of God because of the ignorance that is in them due to the hardening of their hearts. Having lost all sensitivity, they have given themselves over to sensuality so as to indulge in every kind of impurity, with a continual lust for more. (Eph. 4:17–19 NIV)

The loss of sensitivity that Paul is referring to here is the dullness that most people accept as normal. It actually leads us into sin, to sensuality and lust. The deadened soul requires a greater and greater level of stimulation to arouse it. This is, of course, the downward spiral of any addiction. What began as an attraction to *Playboy* ends up for the porn addict in some really horrific stuff. Just look at the progression of television drama over the past thirty years. What we have now would have been considered shocking, even repulsive, to an earlier audience. Networks have to keep adding more sex, more violence, to keep our attention. We have become so sensual. This is why holiness is not numbness; it is sensitivity. It is being *more* attuned to our desires, to what we were truly made for and therefore what we truly want. Our problem is that we've grown quite used to seeking life in all kinds of things other than God.

For example, God wants to be our perfect lover, but instead we seek perfection in human relationships and are disappointed when our lovers cannot love us perfectly. God wants to provide our ultimate security, but we seek our safety in power and possessions and then we find we must continually worry about them. We seek satisfaction of our spiritual longing in a host of ways that may have very little to do with God. (*Addiction and Grace*)

And so May comments, "The more we become accustomed to seeking spiritual satisfaction through things other than God, the more abnormal and stressful it becomes to look for God directly." Our instrument is out of tune from years of misuse. This is where the Law is our help. Everything in you may be saying, "But you don't understand. I *want* to eat that whole box of chocolates (or sleep with my boyfriend, or let my anger really fly). That's what really seems like life to me right now." God says, "I know you do, but it'll kill you in the end. What you think is life is not. That's not the comfort (or the love, or the significance) you are seeking. You'll wind up destroying yourself." The commands of God become our tutor in the healing of our desire. We need the Law because our instrument is out of tune; we're not clear all the time on what it is we *really* desire.

And so the first command comes first. God tells us to love him with all our hearts and all our souls, with all our minds and all our strength. It's not a burden but a rescue, a trail out of the jungles of desire. When we don't look for God as our true life, our desire for him spills over into our other desires, giving them an ultimacy and urgency they were never intended to bear. We become desperate, grasping and arranging and worrying over all kinds of things, and once we get them, they end up ruling us. It's the difference between wants and needs. All we truly need is God. Prone to wander from him, we find we need all sorts of other things. Our desire becomes insatiable because we've taken our longing for the Infinite and placed it upon finite things. God saves us from the whole mimetic mess by turning our hearts back to him.

You may have heard an orchestra tuning up before a concert. It sounds like total chaos—oboes, cello, French horns, dozens of instruments all sounding off, everyone doing his own thing. Trills, groans, whistles, thumps—an absolute cacophony. This is how our desires seem most of the time. But then the first violin plays a long high C, and slowly, all the other instruments join in. They become focused, centered, ready to perform. Such is what happens with the chaos of our desires when we turn our souls to God in worship. All the other desires find their place as we give God his place. That is why the psalmist urges us, "Delight yourself in the LORD and he will give you the desires of your heart" (Ps. 37:4 NIV). Only as we truly delight in God is it safe to give us our desires, for then they are not likely to become idols. And by our delighting in God, he heals our false desires as our souls come true in the light of their Maker. *Worship* becomes the means by which we most deeply heal our desire.

WORSHIP—THE HEART'S HEALER

Henri Nouwen once asked Mother Teresa for spiritual direction. Spend one hour each day in adoration of your Lord, she said, and never do anything you know is wrong. Follow this, and you'll be fine. Such simple, yet profound advice. Worship is the act of the abandoned heart adoring its God. It is the union that we crave. Few of us experience anything like this on a regular basis, let alone for an hour each day. But it is what we need. Desperately. Simply showing up on Sunday is not even close to worship. Neither does singing songs with religious content pass for worship. What counts is *the posture of the soul* involved, the open heart pouring forth its love toward God and communing with him. It is a question of desire.

Worship occurs when we say to God, from the bottom of our hearts, "You are the One whom I desire." As Thomas à Kempis prayed, "There is nothing created that can fully satisfy my desires. Make me one with You in a sure bond of heavenly love, for You alone are sufficient to Your lover, and without You all things are vain and of no substance."

I spent a year in the Psalms at the same time I was resting from the duty of Sunday morning. I wasn't studying them with my head; I was praying them from my heart. It gave me a voice for the cry of my soul—the anguish, the weariness, the joy, the sorrow. It's all there. What is remarkable is that no matter where the poet begins, he almost always ends in worship. This is no coincidence. It is where our journey must lead us. In the most often quoted phrase from Augustine, he says, "Our hearts are restless until they find their rest in Thee." He is referring to desire. Our only hope for rest from the incessant craving of our desire is in God, and us united to him. And so à Kempis prayed, "O faithful soul, make ready thy heart for this Bridegroom." He continued,

Grant me, O most sweet and loving Jesus, to rest in thee above all creatures, above all health and beauty, above all glory and honor, above all power and dignity, above all knowledge and subtlety, above all riches and arts, above all joy and gladness, above all fame and praise, above all sweetness and comfort, above all hope and promise, above all desert and desire . . .

Thou alone art most beautiful and loving, thou alone most noble and glorious above all things, in whom all good things together both perfectly are, and ever have been, and shall be.

The full union, of course, is coming. We rehearse for the wedding now through worship.

CHAPTER ELEVEN

LETTING GO

Grasp not at much for fear thou losest all.
—George Herbert

For Jesus I have gladly suffered the loss of all things.
—The apostle Paul

I f you're coming up from the south, the only way to get into the Lamar Valley in northeast Yellowstone is over Dunraven Pass. It's a narrow, winding road over the flanks of Mount Washburn and in recent years badly in need of repair. Still, I had come so far for this. It was three months after Brent's death, and I had made a sort of pilgrimage to Yellowstone. The last great adventure we shared together was here, fly-fishing among the wolves and bears in the Lamar Valley.

I had returned under the auspices of taking my family on vacation, but I sensed there was a deeper reason. Unbeknownst to them, I was on a pilgrimage, drawn here for a purpose only partially known to me. Down the desolate highways of Wyoming, across the Absarokas, up the Snake River from Jackson Hole, I had followed some inner call. There was much to see along the way, and many side trails explored with my family. But finally, we came to my real goal—the road over Dunraven Pass. It was closed.

The orange-and-white barriers stood there like a prophetic

beast out of a nightmare. ROAD CLOSED. *None shall pass*. It seems the Park Service crews had decided—that morning, with no prior warning—to close the road for repairs for the rest of the season. My journey would end here. I sat at the intersection staring dumbly at the barriers, the engine idling, cars piling up behind me. God began to speak to my sinking heart: *Your journey lies along another path. You've got to let all that go now*. I knew there was no arguing. I didn't even try to put up a fight. I've been known to plow through his barriers in the past, but not now. Remember checkmate? My grip has loosened in recent years, and I knew this was a call to loosen it even more. David Wilcox sings about this moment in "Slipping Through My Fist":

I have drifted down a ways along the shoreline,
I just watched these ropes give way
where they were tied.
I could have reached out quick when the ropes first
slipped, if I had tried,
but I was wondering where the wind was trying to take me
overnight, if I never did resist, and
what strange breezes make a sailor want to
let it come to this,
with lines untied, slipping through my fist.
It is downhill all the way to the ocean,
So of course the river wants to flow.
The river's been here longer,
It's older and stronger and knows where to go.

One thing I have come to embrace is this: we have to let it go. The more comfortable we are with mystery in our journey, the more rest we will know along the way. The Christian life is full of paradox (as if you hadn't noticed). Listen to how Paul describes his experience of the quest: "Sorrowful, yet always rejoicing; poor, yet making many rich; having nothing, and yet possessing everything" (2 Cor. 6:10 NIV). How true this is. If we will remain open to sorrow, we can know joy. Somehow being empty allows us to make others rich. And if we are willing to let go, we'll discover something most surprising—that all is ours. That is why reaching to possess is one danger of which the heart alive must be wary. Those who have given up caring aren't tempted by this. But once we *know* what we want, we must learn the grace of release.

WILLING TO THIRST

There is a widespread belief in the church that to be a Christian somehow satisfies our every desire. As one camp song has it, "I'm inright, outright, upright, downright happy all day long." What complete nonsense! Augustine emphasized, "The whole life of the good Christian is a holy longing. What you desire ardently, as yet you do not see." So, "let us long because we are to be filled . . . That is our life, to be exercised by longing." There's the mystery again. Longing leads to fullness somewhere down the road. Meanwhile, being content is not the same thing as being full.

Paul said he had "learned the secret of being content" (Phil. 4:12 NIV), and many Christians assume he no longer experienced the thirst of his soul. But earlier in the same epistle, the old saint said that he had *not* obtained his soul's desire, or "already been made perfect." Quite the contrary. He described himself as pressing on, "straining toward what is ahead" (Phil. 3:12–14 NIV). These are not the words of a man who no longer experienced longing because he had arrived. They are the account of a man propelled on his life quest by his desire.

Contentment is not freedom *from* desire, but freedom *of* desire. Being content is not pretending that everything is the way you wish it would be; it is not acting as though you have no wishes. Rather, it is no longer being *ruled* by your desires.

The fact is, at this point in our journey, we have only three options: (1) to be alive and thirsty, (2) to be dead, or (3) to be addicted. There are no other choices. Most of the world lives in addiction; most of the church has chosen deadness. The Christian is called to the life of holy longing. But we don't like to stay there. A. W. Tozer perceived that "there is within the human heart a tough, fibrous root of fallen life whose nature is to possess, always to possess." And why do we seek to possess? So that we do not have to live in thirst, trusting our hearts each day to the goodness of God. To live in thirst is to live with an ache. Every addiction comes from the attempt to get rid of the ache. How is it possible to satisfy an insatiable desire? Merely trying sets us on an unending chase that leads us farther and farther from home.

And thus life passes away. Men combat with a thousand difficulties for the sake of repose, and as soon as they have overcome them all, repose becomes intolerable. For their thoughts are turned either on existing evils, or on such as are impending. And when secure on all sides from danger, their inherent disquietude, destitute of objects it might just fix upon, still continues to shoot from the heart, its native soil, and overspreads the soul with its venom.

What can this incessant craving, and this impotence of attainment mean, unless there was once a happiness belonging to man, of which only the faintest traces remain, in that void which he attempts to fill with everything within his reach? But it is in vain he seeks from absent objects the relief things present cannot give, and which neither of them can give; because, in a soul that will live forever, there is an infinite void that nothing can fill, but an infinite unchangeable being. (*Pensées*)

You can be satisfied, says Pascal; you just can't be sated. There is great joy in a glass of cabernet; the whole bottle is another story. Intimate conversation satisfies a different thirst, but how awful to try to arrange for it again the next night and the night after that. The Israelites tried to hoard the manna—and it crawled with maggots. Our soul's insatiable desire becomes the venom Pascal warns of when it demands its fill here and now, through the otherwise beautiful and good gifts of our lives.

God grants us so much of our heart's desire as we delight in him: "You open your hand and satisfy the desires of every living thing" (Ps. 145:16 NIV). Not always, not on demand, but certainly more than we deserve. God delights to give good gifts to his beloved. But that old root would have us shift once more from giver to gift, and seek our rest through being full. This is the turn we must be vigilant to see, watching over our hearts with loving care. In his lovely poem "The Size," George Herbert prays,

> Content thee, greedie heart.
> Modest and moderate joys to those, that have
> Title to more hereafter when they part,
> Are passing brave.
>
> If thou hast wherewithall to spice a draught,
> When griefs prevail;
> And for the future time art heir
> To th' Isle of spices, is't not fair?
> To be in both worlds full
> Is more than God was, who was hungrie here.

Remember, pleasure is often more about drugging ourselves than it is about enjoying ourselves. And the things we do to avoid the ache are always worse in the end than the ache itself. I think of Jamie, a bright and energetic young woman who has tried so hard to know the right thing to do in every situation. She has tied herself in knots trying to figure out the will of God, solve all the theological quandaries, never miss a beat. She wrote to me recently, "I am caught in a tangle of trying to *do*, trying to live *right*. I don't know how to not think or worry or control. I don't know how to let go." It's driving her absolutely crazy. (Didn't Chesterton warn us, "Poets do not go mad; but chess-players do"?) Why can't she let go? "I want to predict what the Lord is going to do, so that it doesn't hurt so bad when it happens." Jamie grasped onto perfectionism to avoid pain and disappointment. It only made matters worse. As Carl Jung asserted, "Neurosis is always a substitute for legitimate suffering." So what do we do? How do we live with desire we cannot take care of and heartache we cannot prevent? We groan and wait.

WHAT HOPE FEELS LIKE

We know that the whole creation has been groaning as in the pains of childbirth right up to the present time. Not only so, but we ourselves, who have the firstfruits of the Spirit, groan inwardly as we wait eagerly for our adoption as sons, the redemption of our bodies. For in this hope we were saved. But hope that is seen is no hope at all. Who hopes for what he already has? But if we hope for what we do not yet have, we wait for it patiently. (Rom. 8:22–25 NIV)

Amazing. Paul is passing along to us the secret of the sojourning heart. We live in hope, and he says hoping is waiting. And groaning. When was the last time you heard that in a sermon or the title for a new book? *You, Too, Can Groan Inwardly While You Wait Eagerly!* Everything I've seen lately offers a sure-fire way to "get what you want." How to be a success at work. How to be a success at love. How to succeed in work *and* love at the same time.

Here are questions to ask yourself to see if you are a pilgrim or an arranger: What am I waiting for? Is there anything I ardently desire that I am doing nothing to secure? The first time I asked myself, I couldn't name a thing. There were many things I was working on, or fretting over, or had given up wanting. I am thankful that was some time ago. Things are different now. Now I wonder, What am I still arranging for? I should like to let it go too.

WAITING

To wait is to learn the spiritual grace of *detachment*, the freedom of desire. Not the absence of desire, but desire at rest. St. John of the Cross lamented that "the desires weary and fatigue the soul; for they are like restless and discontented children, who are ever demanding this or that from their mother, and are never contented." Detachment is coming to the place where those demanding children are at peace. As King David said,

> I have stilled and quieted my soul;
> > like a weaned child with its mother,
> > like a weaned child is my soul within me.
> > > (Ps 131:2 NIV)

Such a beautiful picture, a young one leaning against her mother's breast. There is no fussing, no insistent tears. She has learned to wait.

The word *detachment* might evoke wrong impressions. It is not a cold and indifferent attitude; not at all. May writes, "An authentic spiritual understanding of detachment devalues neither desire nor the objects of desire." Instead, it "aims at correcting one's own anxious grasping in order to free oneself for committed relationship to God."

Bethann told me this beautiful story after we both attended a conference in Denver: "After nine days of being with twelve hundred people, I wanted to breathe, to be alone, and to be free." So she went antique shopping downtown. The first shop she stepped into was very upscale. "It felt more like a museum or even cathedral than a shop. I felt out of place. Obviously, I couldn't buy anything here. I clutched my purse closely to make sure that I didn't knock anything over." Enormous English armoires, French marble fireplaces, an $18,000 Roman bathtub. Reaching the back of the store, Bethann turned into a narrow passage between pieces and was captivated by a stained glass window. "It must have come from a chalet in France. It was propped up against a window and the light that came through it seemed somehow purified; the shades of soft yellow and blue and rose flowing from an urn of profuse flowers with ribbons elegantly fluttering away. I don't know how long I stood there with my mouth open. It made my heart swell and fill and ache at the same time." Her mind began to race: How could she possess it for her own? But at $8,000, the window was beyond hoping for. "Resignation, hopelessness, and anger followed. Then out of nowhere, I rebounded. I *will* have it in my home—in heaven. Some guy making six figures may be able to have it for a few years, but I'll have it forever." It was the first time, she told me, that she saw her desires filled in the coming kingdom. *I've got the better end of the deal,* she said to herself and walked out.

As Thomas à Kempis declared, "Wait a little while, O my

soul, wait for the divine promise, and thou shalt have abundance of all good things in heaven." In this posture we discover that, indeed, we are expanded by longing. Something grows in us, a capacity if you will, for life and love and God. I think of Romans 8:24–25: "That is why waiting does not diminish us, any more than waiting diminishes a pregnant mother. We are enlarged in the waiting. We, of course, don't see what is enlarging us. But the longer we wait, the larger we become, and the more joyful our expectancy" (*The Message*). There is actually a sweet pain in longing if we will let it draw our hearts homeward.

AND GROANING

When I turned away from those barriers to the Lamar Valley, I accepted that I could not recover what had been lost. Not yet. My journey now lies along another path. And so we retreated from the road over Dunraven Pass, left Yellowstone through the south gate, and descended into the Tetons, staying there for several nights.

One morning I woke early and could not get back to sleep. My soul was agitated, restless. After what seemed like an hour of tossing and turning, I rose and slipped out of the cabin to take a walk. Waves of grief began to sweep over my soul. But it was not all about Brent or even primarily about him. His death was the lance that pierced the wound of all the ungrieved grief of my life. Sorrows from my marriage, from college days, from wounds I received as a child—all of them poured forth through this place of release. Why had I waited so many years to shed these tears? As I wept, I realized that Paul was absolutely right. How can we live without groaning? If we do not give our ache a voice, it doesn't go away. It becomes the undercurrent of our addictions. Pleasure becomes necessary in larger and larger doses, like morphine.

The paradox of grief is that it is healing; it somehow restores our souls, when all the while we thought it would leave us in despair. Control is the enemy; grief is our friend. Jamie came to realize this when her boyfriend decided he did not know if he could love her and broke off their relationship. She wrote,

> The problem is that I was already choosing to love him. How hard it was for me to let down the walls and care—risk. And it isn't that I did anything wrong in dating, so there is nothing that I can say I should have done or should not have done, besides love him. Oh, I don't know if this is making any sense, but through the breakup I have been real. I have not done my usual "cover up and pretend that I never cared in the first place." Instead I have hurt, I have embraced the pain and the reality that there is nothing that I can do besides wait for the healing. Embracing the pain has brought me to a place of more complete healing than I feel I could have known otherwise.

As she let go of her controlling, something better took its place—mourning. When the ministry of the Messiah is described in Isaiah 61, comfort for those who mourn and healing for the brokenhearted are placed at the center of his mission. None of this makes sense until we admit our brokenheartedness and give our sorrow a voice in mourning. Only then will we know his comfort. Until then, they are nice, religious-sounding words.

Solomon said that it is better to go to a house of mourning than it is to a house of feasting. I never understood this; I wrote it off as the pessimism of a depressed man. Now I think I know what he meant. Grief is good. It is cleansing. It undoes my world—and that is the best part of it. I need to be undone; simply undone. No regrouping. We need to mourn; it is the only way our hearts can remain both free and alive in this world. Why? Because it, like

nothing else, puts a stop to the constant striving. Grief is the anti-
dote to the incessant possessive demand within.

Another friend, Deborah, wrote,

How do I live in the world I have with my woundedness? How
do I live as an alive woman in the world I have? I am so grateful
every time God speaks deeply to my heart. I started to acknowledge my deep, deep loneliness, and when I did, everything has
been happening in a rush, like a river freed, fast and tumultuous.
I've been crying and it just keeps going—the kind of tears and
feelings of grief that I've cried when family members have died
. . . but it's oh so good, because it is also a feeling of being alive
to who God made me to be and it's acknowledging the truth of
how I see life and experience life.

> Those who sow in tears
>   will reap with songs of joy.
> He who goes out weeping,
>   carrying seed to sow,
> will return with songs of joy,
>   carrying sheaves with him.
>   (Ps. 126:5-6 NIV)

I believe we must add two spiritual disciplines to everyday life.
The first is worship. We must adore God deliberately, regularly.
The other is grief. We must allow a time for sorrow to do our own
personal sowing. I see no other way to care for our hearts.

Now making time to grieve might seem strange to you. "But I
don't feel grief or sorrow at all." Just because we do not feel it
doesn't mean it is not there. Our pleasant experience may be the
result of the thousand distractions that fill our waking moments.
Kierkegaard said that despair has become so rare not because the

human race is doing suddenly better, but because we so effectively push it away. This is the "sickness unto death," to despair without ever despairing, to mourn without ever mourning.

I've found, therefore, that quite often grief has to sneak up on us, surprise us during our day. It may come through a song you hear or a movie you see. It may come as you choose to allow your soul twenty minutes of quiet during your lunch hour. Sometimes a small disappointment can be the door into a room of grief you never knew was there. However unexpectedly grief shows up, let us accept it as a welcome visitor.

This is the last journal entry I made *before* going to the mountains with Brent, the weekend he was killed: *Life is loss and I must grieve regularly, so as to give up trying to possess. I will not arrive in the golden place until I am home with God.* The last thing Jesus said to me before that weekend was, *Don't run from the suffering. Embrace it.* I had no idea what was coming. I had no idea how prophetic those words would be. I knew only the truth of them from the journey thus far. They are truer now.

LET BEAUTY HAVE ITS SAY

What can I possibly say to her? How can I begin to restore hope to her life? This is what was going through my mind as I listened to Kathleen. It was partly about being raped, and partly about the tensions in her marriage remaining years after, that she had come to see me. I wondered, *What can I offer this woman? What can I say to one who has known such terrible evil?* We sat in my office on a cold winter afternoon; outside all was gray. Perhaps that's the reason I first noticed the little flowers embroidered on the collar of her denim shirt. As she told me her tragic story, my eye kept coming back to those graceful little bouquets. Maybe I was surprised by them, but somehow I felt they were the clue to her restoration.

Kathleen finished her story, and we sat in silence. After a few moments, I couldn't help mentioning the flowers. "Oh," she said. "Ever since the rape, beauty has meant the world to me. No one seemed to understand why. Sometimes I would spend hours just gazing at my garden and the woods behind my house. Only beauty helps."

I understand completely. As the shock of Brent's death began to wear off, the searing pain of intense grief took its place. It was too difficult to read my Bible. Conversation required more than I was able to give. Frankly, I didn't want to talk to anyone, not even God. The only thing that helped was my wife's flower garden. The solace I found there was like nothing else on earth. I wrote in my journal, *Sitting outside this evening, the Shasta daisies swaying in the gentle breeze on their long stems, the aspens shimmering without light, the full moon rising over the pine-crested bluff . . . only beauty speaks what I need to hear. Only beauty helps.*

Simone Weil was absolutely right—beauty and affliction are the only two things that can pierce our hearts. Because this is so true, we must have a measure of beauty in our lives proportionate to our affliction. No, more. Much more. Is this not God's prescription for us? Just take a look around. The sights and sounds, the aromas and sensations—the world is overflowing with beauty. God seems to be rather enamored with it. Gloriously wasteful. Apparently, he feels that there ought to be plenty of it in our lives.

I am at a loss to say what I want to say regarding beauty. Somehow, that is as it ought to be. Our experience of beauty transcends our ability to speak about it, for its magic lies beyond the power of words. Wordsworth penned these lines:

> Thanks to the human heart by which we live,
> Thanks to its tenderness, its joys, and fears,

To me the meanest flower that blows can give
Thoughts that do often lie too deep for tears.

I want to speak of beauty's healing power, of how it comforts and soothes, yet also how it stirs us, how it moves and inspires. All that sounds ridiculous. You know your own experiences of beauty. Let me call upon them then. Think of your favorite music, or tapestry, or landscape. "We have had a couple of inspiring sunsets this week." A dear friend sent this in an E-mail: "It was as if the seams of our atmosphere split for a bit of heaven to plunge into the sea. I stood and applauded . . . simultaneously I wanted to kneel and weep." Yes—that's it. All I want to do is validate those irreplaceable moments, lift any obstacle you may have to filling your life with greater and greater amounts of beauty.

We need not fear indulging here. The experience of beauty is unique to all the other pleasures in this: there is no possessive quality to it. Just because you love the landscape doesn't mean you have to acquire the real estate. Simply to behold the flower is enough; there is nothing in me that wants to consume it. Beauty is the closest thing we have to fullness without possessing on this side of eternity. It heralds the Great Restoration. Perhaps that is why it is so healing—beauty is pure gift. It helps us in our letting go.

SURRENDER

The time has come for us to quit playing chess with God over our lives. We cannot win, but we can delay the victory, dragging on the pain of grasping and the poison of possessing. You see, there are two kinds of losses in life. The first is shared by all mankind—the losses that come to us. Call them what you will—accidents, fate, acts of God. The point is that we have no control over them. We do not determine when, where, what, or even how. There is no predicting these losses; they happen *to* us. We choose only how we respond. The second kind is known only to the pilgrim. They are losses that we *choose.* A chosen loss is different from repentance, when we give up something that was never ours to have. With a chosen loss, we place on the altar something very dear to us, something innocent, whose only danger is in its goodness, that we might come to love it too much. It is the act of *consecration,* where little by little or all at once, we give over our lives to the only One who can truly keep them.

Spiritual surrender is not resignation. It is not choosing to care no longer. Nor is it Eastern mysticism, an attempt to get beyond the suffering of this life by going completely numb. As my dear friend Jan describes, "It is surrender *with* desire, or *in* desire." Desire is still present, felt, welcomed even. But the will to secure is made subject to the divine will in an act of abandoned trust. Think of Jesus in the Garden of Gethsemane. Frederick Buechner has suggested that we contrast him with a picture we have of Buddha, so that we might see the difference of true surrender:

Buddha sits enthroned beneath the Bo-tree in the lotus position. His lips are faintly parted in the smile of one who has passed beyond every power in earth or heaven to touch him. "He who loves fifty has fifty woes, he who loves ten has ten woes, he who loves none has no woes," he has said. His eyes are closed.

Christ, on the other hand, stands in the garden of Gethsemane, angular, beleaguered. His face is lost in the shadows so that you can't even see his lips, and before all the powers on earth or heaven he is powerless. "This is my commandment, that you love one another as I have loved you," he has said. (*Now and Then*)

Christ is weeping freely; his prayers are marked by loud cries and tears. He makes it very, very clear what he desires. Not once, but three times he begs his Father to remove this awful cup from him: "Yet not my will, but thine be done." He surrenders with desire, in desire. Making himself poor, he opens up to us the treasures of heaven. Buddha abandons his desire; Christ surrenders his will. It is no small difference.

True surrender is not an easy out, calling it quits early in the game. This kind of surrender comes only *after* the night of wrestling. It comes only after we open our hearts to care deeply. Then we choose to surrender, or give over, our deepest desires to God. And with them we give over our hearts, our deepest selves. The freedom and beauty and rest that follow are among the greatest of all surprises.

After he lost his son, Wolterstorff did not remain passive: he wept; he railed; he lamented. I suppose it was his own Gethsemane. That trail of tears brought him to a place of true surrender. This is how he describes it:

> Let me try again. All these things I still recognize. I remember delighting in them—trees, art, house, music, pink morning sky, work well done, flowers, books. I still delight in them. I'm still grateful. But the zest is gone. The passion is cooled, the striving is quieted, the longing stilled. My attachment is loosened. No longer do I set my heart on them. I can do without them. They don't matter. Instead of rowing, I float. The joy that comes my way I savor. But the seeking, the clutching, the aiming is gone. (*Lament for a Son*)

I tasted this wonderful freedom a few months ago, canoeing on a high mountain lake. My boys had already gone in for the day, and so I was alone in the canoe, paddling across this beautiful lake at dusk. That was when the trout began to rise. The surface of the water was serene in the little cove I had found, and the dimples made by feeding rainbows were too numerous to count. It is the moment fly fishermen dream about. I set down the paddle and picked up my rod to begin casting. As the line unfurled, my fly alighted gently on the water in the middle of a dozen rise-rings. First one, then two trout took my offering. I knew that if the fish continued to rise, I would have my fill before it became too dark to fish anymore. But then, a gentle breeze began to blow down the valley. It was cool and fragrant and refreshing, and though it was soft, I noticed it was strong enough to carry my canoe along. A tremor of anxiety passed through me, for I knew I could not fish and paddle at the same time. To stay in this little cove, among the rising trout, I would have to put down the rod and pick up the paddle.

I smiled and set down the rod. But I didn't take up the paddle. I let my hands rest along the gunwales and let the gentle breeze take me away, out across the surface of the lake. And as I drifted, I drank in the beauty of the mountain peaks around me, and the golden quality of the fading light, and the joy of the freedom of my desire. A little voice reminded me that fish were rising back in the cove.

But I was wondering where the wind was trying to take me
overnight, if I never did resist, and
what strange breezes make a sailor want to
let it come to this,
with lines untied, slipping through my fist.

CHAPTER TWELVE

KEEPING HEART—
TO THE END

Remember thee!
Yea, from the table of my memory
I'll wipe away all trivial fond records . . .
And thy commandment all alone shall live
Within the book and volume of my brain
Unmix'd with baser matter.

—Hamlet

Sometimes I wake, and, lo, I have forgot.
—George MacDonald

But every now and anon a trumpet sounds from the hid bat-
tlements of eternity.
—Francis Thompson

Gabriel García Marquez's novel *One Hundred Years of Solitude* chronicles the life of the little Mexican town of Macondo and the families who call it home. At one point in their domestic journey, a plague of insomnia strikes the little village. The residents go weeks, then months without sleep. They begin to lose vital faculties. First to go is the memory—no small aspect for living. Even the simplest and most common household goods appear foreign, unfamiliar, forgotten. Aureliano, the silversmith, is working in his shop one day when he realizes he cannot remember the name for the little anvil he uses. His father, Jose, tells him the name.

Aureliano wrote the name on a piece of paper that he pasted to the base of the small anvil: *stake*. In that way he was sure of not forgetting it in the future. It did not occur to him that this was the first manifestation of a loss of memory, because the object had a difficult name to remember. But a few days later he discovered that he had trouble remembering almost every object in the laboratory. Then he marked them with their respective names so that all he had to do was read the inscription in order to identify them . . . [Jose] put it into practice all through the house and later on imposed it on the whole village. With an inked brush he marked everything with its name: *table, chair, clock, door, wall, bed, pan*. He went to the corral and marked the animals and plants: *cow, goat, pig, hen, cassava, caladium, banana*. Little by little, studying the infinite possibilities of a loss of memory, he realized that the day might come when things would be recognized by their inscriptions but that no one would remember their use. Then he was more explicit. The sign that he hung on the neck of the cow was an exemplary proof of the way in which the inhabitants of Macondo were prepared to fight against loss of memory: *This is the cow. She must be milked every morning so that she will produce milk, and the milk must be boiled in order to be mixed with coffee to make coffee and milk.*

. . . At the beginning of the road into the swamp they put up a sign that said *Macondo* and another larger one on the main street that said *God exists*.

OUR WORST ENEMY

The first time I read this story I simply laughed. But it haunted me, and on a second reading I began to realize that it's my story too. I said to myself, *It's not a bad plan. Right above my bed I think I shall hang a sign that says, GOD EXISTS.* You see, I wake most mornings an unbeliever. It seems that during the night, I slip into forgetfulness, and by the time the new day comes, I am lost. The deep and precious truths that God has brought to me over the years and even just yesterday seem a thousand miles away. It doesn't happen every morning, but enough to make it an ongoing reality. And I know I am not alone in this. As MacDonald confessed in *Diary of an Old Soul,*

> Sometimes I wake, and lo, I have forgot,
> And drifted out upon an ebbing sea!
> My soul that was at rest now resteth not,
> For I am with myself and not with thee;
> Truth seems a blind moon in a glaring morn,
> Where nothing is but sick-heart vanity.

Virtually every person I've ever counseled follows a similar pattern. Over the course of our time together, some wonderful things begin to happen. Not necessarily at first, and never on command, but God shows up. The lights turn on for these people; their heart is lifted; grateful tears flow. Suddenly, faith, hope, and love seem the only way to live. And I nearly dread the next session. When they return the following week, it is as though it never happened. The marvelous day is a distant memory. Life is hard, God is distant, and love is foolish. All is forgotten; all is sick-heart vanity. I want to grab them and shake them into sense, shouting, "Don't you *remember*? Why did you let it slip away?" Wisdom has kept me restrained so far.

Forgetting is no small problem. Of all the enemies our hearts must face, this may be the worst because it is insidious. Forgetfulness does not come against us like an enemy in full battle formation, banners waving. Nor does it come temptingly, seductively, the lady in red. It works slowly, commonly, unnoticed. My wife had a beautiful climbing rose vine that began to fill an arbor in her garden. We enjoyed the red blossoms it produced every summer. But last year, something happened. The vine suddenly turned brown, dropped its flowers, and died within the course of a week. After all that loving care we couldn't figure out what went wrong. A call to the nursery revealed that a worm had gotten into the stalk of the vine and eaten away at the life from the inside. Such is the work of forgetfulness. It cuts us off from our Life so slowly, we barely notice, until one day the blooms of our faith are suddenly gone.

BE FOREWARNED

We're certainly warned about forgetfulness in Scripture, both in word and by example. In the Old Testament, the pattern is so predictable, we come to expect it. God delivers his people from the cruel whips of Egypt by a stunning display of his power and his care—the plagues, the Passover, the Red Sea. The Israelites celebrate with singing and dancing. Three days later, they are complaining about the water supply. God provides sweet water from the bitter desert springs of Marah. They complain about the food. God drops breakfast out of the sky, every morning. Then it's the water again. God provides it from a rock. Enemies attack; God delivers. On and on it goes, for forty years. As they stand on the brink of the promised land, God issues a final warning: "Only be careful, and watch yourselves closely so that you do not forget the things your eyes have seen or *let them slip from your heart* as long as you live" (Deut. 4:9 NIV, emphasis added).

They do, of course, let it slip from their hearts. All of it. This becomes the pattern for the entire history of Israel. God shows up; he does amazing things; the people rejoice. Then they forget and go whoring after other gods. They fall under calamity and cry out for deliverance. God shows up; he does amazing things; the people rejoice—you get the picture. Round and round and round we go; where she stops, nobody knows.

And like that of the people of Macondo, their story is our story. Things aren't changed much in the New Testament, but the contrast is greater, and the stakes are even higher. God shows up *in person*, and before he leaves, he gives us the sacraments along with this plea: *Do this to remember me.*

They don't—remember him, that is. Paul is "shocked" by the Galatians: they are "turning away so soon from God, who in his love and mercy called you to share the eternal life he gives through Christ" (1:6 NLT). He has to send Timothy to the Corinthians, to "remind you of what I teach about Christ Jesus in all the churches wherever I go" (1 Cor 4:17 NLT). Peter, who knew firsthand the grief that comes from forgetting, writes his letters to combat this cancer of the soul: "So keep a firm grip on the faith. The suffering won't last forever. It won't be long before this generous God who has great plans for us in Christ—eternal and glorious plans they are!—will have you put together and on your feet for good" (1 Peter 5:10 *The Message*).

It happens to the best of us. Brent and I were having coffee with a pastor from Denver, whose wife was greatly helped by the things we wrote about in *The Sacred Romance.* He told us of her long exile in the desert of her soul, which was deepened by a bout with depression. Our words about life and God and the journey of the heart had been the means by which God had brought life to her parched heart. Her husband was truly grateful for the book, and he thanked us again and again for writing it. You would think both of us would have been quite moved. Authors live to hear such things. But Brent's comment betrayed a deeper reality: "Really? You mean, it's *true*?"

WHAT WILL WE CLING TO?

Life is a journey of the heart that requires the mind—not the other way around. The church sometimes gets this backward and makes knowing the right things the center of life. It's not; the heart is the center of life. Desire is always where the action is. However, staying alive to our desire is not enough; we know that only too well. We must bring the *truth* into our hearts to guard and to guide our desire; this is the other half of our mission. With a recovery of heart and soul taking place in many quarters, my fear now is that we will abandon the pursuit of truth and try to base our journey on our feelings and intuition. "Follow your heart" is becoming a popular message in our culture. Or as Sting sings, "Trust your soul." It will not work. Our spiritual fathers and mothers knew this only too well. In *The Imitation of Christ*, Thomas à Kempis warned, "Our own opinion and our own sense do often deceive us, and they discern but little." We must cling to the truth for dear life. And so our spiritual forbears urged us to bring *both* heart and mind together. As James Houston says in *The Heart's Desire*,

In medieval Christian thought, the idea of learning by heart was something that went far deeper than mathematical tables. It meant the re-orientation of one's life, by what Benedict called *haga*, bringing the thoughts of the mind into the heart, so that one's whole person stood in the presence of God. A Russian monk of the nineteenth century, Theophan the Recluse, gives weight to a similar idea: "The principal thing is to stand before God with the intellect in the heart, and to go on standing before him unceasingly day and night, until the end of life."

Now, not all truths help us descend with the mind into the heart. There is a way of talking about the truth that can actually deaden our hearts. Most of us were raised in the modern era, the age of reason and science. We came to believe that truth is best discovered in the scientific method—dissection. And if you will remember high school biology, we discovered quite a bit about the cat on the table before us—its respiratory system, its muscles and sinews, and all that. Only when the experiment is finished, you have nothing like a cat left at all. You have facts about a cat, but you are far from the real thing anymore. The coy, playful, aloof creature who stands waiting to be let out and walks back into the room once you've risen to open the door—the *living cat*—is gone.

Let me give another example: what is the truth of a kiss? Technically, in a modernistic sense, it is two sets of mandibles pressing together for a certain duration of time. Those of you who have experienced the wonders of a kiss will know that while true, this description is so untrue. It takes away everything beautiful and mysterious and passionate and intimate and leaves you with an icy cold fact. Those who know kissing feel robbed; those who don't are apt to say, "If that's what kissing is all about, I think I'd rather not."

We've done the same thing to theology. We have dissected God, and man, and the gospel, and we have thousands, if not millions, of facts—all of it quite dead. It's not that these insights aren't true; it's that they no longer speak. I could tell you a few facts about God, for example. He is omniscient, omnipotent, and immutable. There—don't you feel closer to him? All our statements about God forget that he is a person, and as Tozer says, "In the deep of His mighty nature He thinks, wills, enjoys, feels, loves, desires and suffers as any other person may." How do we get to know a person? Through stories. All the wild and sad and courageous tales that we tell—they are what reveal us to others. We must return to the Scriptures for the story that it is and stop approaching it as if it is an encyclopedia, looking for "tips and techniques."

Reminders of the story are everywhere—in films and novels, in children's fairy tales, in the natural world around us, and in the stories of our own lives. In fact, every story or movie or song or poem that has ever stirred your soul is telling you something you need to know about the Sacred Romance. Even nature is crying out to us of God's great heart and the drama that is unfolding. Sunrise and sunset tell the tale every day, remembering Eden's glory, prophesying Eden's return. These are the trumpet calls from the "hid battlements of eternity." We must capture them like precious treasure, and hold them close to our hearts.

HOW TO CLING

People tie strings around their fingers to offset forgetfulness. God told the Jews to bind what he told them to their foreheads. Some of them took him literally and strapped a little box to the brow in which they carried sections of Scripture. I used to read this with a sense of the ridiculous; now I read it with empathy. I need it strapped right there in front of me, every single day. *God exists.*

Blaise Pascal took it a step farther. On the night of his conversion to Christ, November 23, 1654, he penned these words to capture his encounter with the living God:

Fire. The God of Abraham, the God of Isaac, the God of Jacob . . . Certainty, Certainty, emotion, joy, peace, God of Jesus Christ. *Deum meum et Deum vestrum*, Thy God shall be my God. Oblivion of the world and of everything except God. Joy, Joy, Joy, tears of Joy!

When he died, they found this memorial sewn into his jacket, next to his heart. He had kept it there from the day of his conversion until his last breath.

We must do something similar if we are to keep our hearts with us to the end. For we lose the story every day. It is continually being stolen from us by the evil one—the ultimate deconstructionist. He twists and spins and pulls apart the truth until the fragments we have left are unrecognizable. Or we lose it ourselves in the marketplace of Vanity Fair. Bombarded by thousands of messages each day, every one of them marked urgent, we leave behind the truly important things, the only refuge for our hearts.

I remember a story from my childhood about a little pack rat named Put-it, Pick-it. He ventures out each morning with an important task to do, but then something catches his eye. It is a piece of blue glass. He drops what he is carrying and picks up the glass, determined to bring it home to show his mother. How proud she will be! Along the path, a silver sheen reflects the desert sun. He stops for a closer look. The glass is left behind, for now he has something even better—a bottle cap. On and on it goes. By the time he gets home, the true treasure is long gone.

We must be more intentional about holding on to the truth. The spiritual pilgrims who aligned themselves with St. Benedict took this task seriously—far more seriously than we do, I'm afraid. A typical day in the lives of Benedictine monks began in the middle of the night, when they arose for the Night Office. No less than twelve psalms would be said, together with three

Scripture readings, several hymns, and prayers. Sunrise brought the Morning Office, followed by six other breaks during the labors of the day for remembering: Prime, Terce, Sext, None, Vespers, and Compline in the evening. Seven times a day set aside for prayer and the recitation of psalms. Together with their night vigil, more than twenty-nine psalms would be said, not to mention numerous lessons, verses, prayers, and hymns.

Now, I'm not suggesting that we all adopt the Rule of Benedict. But think about this: these men left the distractions of the world to focus entirely on God. They lived in an environment *designed* to keep them standing before God, and what did they discover? They needed reminders every hour of the day and night! Do we, who live in the hostile chaos of the world, think we can do with an occasional visit? "Hey, Lord, I know it's been a while, but . . . um . . . thanks for being here and please help me get through this day." We are kidding ourselves if we think we can keep heart without a constant turning to the truth. So let me suggest a bit of monastic wisdom for contemporary pilgrims.

First, you must reduce the constant noise of your life. Turn off the television; it is an enemy of your heart. Having one is like inviting Vanity Fair to set up shop in your home. The whole operation runs on mimetic passion, a continual assault on your desire. Even the news is a problem because of its artificial importance. Have you noticed? Every night there's an urgency to the stories; that's what they have to do to sell the news. But if everything is urgent, then nothing is. I believe Thoreau said, "Don't read the Times; read the eternities." Given the pace of our lives, I doubt we have room for both. Simply unplug from all the clamor, and make room for eternity in your life. In *The Wisdom of the Desert*, Thomas Merton reminds us of the early Christians who fled to the deserts south of Palestine in order to draw near to God. They saw society "as a shipwreck from which every single man had to swim for his life." They believed that to "let oneself drift along, passively accepting the tenets and values of what they knew as society, was purely and simply a disaster."

TREASURES FOR OUR HEARTS

After the shepherds learn about the birth of Christ from the angels, they seek and find the Babe, lying in a manger. The whole village is astounded by their report, but Mary, we are told, "treasured up all these things and pondered them in her heart" (Luke 2:19 NIV). Later, when the boy Jesus is found in the temple holding forth with the religious leaders, we are told again that everyone is quite amazed. "But his mother treasured all these things in her heart" (Luke 2:51 NIV). It is more than a touching story of a mother's love; Mary is going to need those treasures when the tide turns against her son. At her darkest hour, when a sword pierces her soul, she does not lose heart. I believe this is why.

So if you do not have a way of seizing what God is speaking to you, begin journaling. Each year I take up a new journal in which to capture my heart's journey. *Journals* chronicle *journeys;* this is far different from simply recording the day's events in a diary, or worse still, the weekly goal sheets of the popular schedulers. A journal is about the interior life. At the back there is a section I have entitled "This New Day." There I am writing the central truths I must return to each morning (at least) to guide my desire home. My journal will be filled with all the twists and turns a year can bring, but here is the place I can go for the *interpretation* of the events and emotions and experiences. Like the Benedictines, we must keep before us the deepest truths—morning, noon, and night.

As my friend Craig and I sat in the warm sun, eating lunch

beside Four Mile Canyon, he picked up Pascal and read these words out loud: "It is awful to feel that everything we possess is hastening away, and to persist in our attachment, without being anxious, to examine if there is no object attainable that will be permanent." It was Thursday afternoon; that evening, our men's retreat was to begin. We had come up early to fish and to scout the area we would use for our rock-climbing sessions. Brent and the other guys would meet us later at the ranch.

The canyon is a beautiful place, with a lovely creek meandering through a meadow, framed on both sides by the high rock walls. It seemed strange to be talking about life slipping away when so much promise was in the air. A wonderful weekend lay ahead with some great men, doing the things I love best. I did not know why Craig had opened the *Pensées*, nor did I know the real story that was about to unfold. I would later realize that these were prophetic words, spoken to us by God at the opening of a very different scene.

God is speaking to us more often than we imagine. These are the treasures we must hide in our own hearts—sew them into our jackets if need be—for the dark hours that may come. As Buechner points out, "His word to us is both recoverable and precious beyond telling." And so I share a few of my notes, only in the hope that they will stir you to capture and hang on to the words and images that bring the romance back to you each new day:

- *The story continues.* This simple statement reminds me that life is unfolding, that we are headed somewhere, that the story is moving toward its happy ending. "What's past is prologue," as Shakespeare said. No event is the final word. Several weeks after Brent died, as I was walking from my car to my office, I said to myself, *The story has taken a tragic turn.* Somehow it mattered immensely to say it this way because it reminded me of all the tragic stories I have known and how they made me feel, how the heroes of those stories faced their tragedies, and so it gave weight to what I was living through. But it also kept me from despair because I found the moment in its context, not a random event but as Brent would often say, "A love affair in the midst of a life-and-death struggle." I was able to allow my heart to know it is not the end—the story continues. Dan Allender notes, "Faith increases to the degree we are aware of, caught up in, enthralled by, and participating in His and our story."

- *It can't be done.* By this I remember that I can't arrange for the life I prize. I am not fully healed yet of my addictions and my tendency—which seems so second nature—to arrange for my own little Eden now. To say again and again, "It can't be done," does not discourage me; quite the contrary, it frees my heart from the grasping and plotting and fretting over my life, which always accompany arranging. It reminds me to let it go. It breaks the power of the spell the evil one is trying to weave around us.

- *It is coming.* Oh, how I forget this most of all. How easy it is to slip back into thinking that it's now or never; that if it's not here, it's not at all. The life I prize is coming. The very thing that I am aching for now, missing now, seeking now in other things is exactly what's coming to me. This is how I interpret the promises that seem to be coming through the good and beautiful gifts we have now. As you raise your glass of wine, toast to the banquet to come; as you see anything beautiful you'd like to have (Bethann's window), say to yourself, *In a little while it shall be mine forever;* as you make love, remember it is rehearsal for the Grand Affair. That way your heart will not be trapped there. I recall the end of MacDonald's novel *Phantastes*: "A great good is coming—is coming—is coming to thee."

- *Battle and journey.* We are at war, and the bloody battle is over our hearts. I am astounded how few Christians see this, how little they protect their hearts. We act as though we live in a sleepy little town during peacetime. We don't. We live in the spiritual equivalent of Bosnia or Beirut. Act like it. Watch over your heart. Don't let just anything in; don't let it go just anywhere. *What's this going to do to my heart?* is a question that I ask in every situation.

  And thinking of life as a journey reminds me to stop trying to set up camp and call it home. It allows me to see life as process, with completion somewhere down the road. Thus I am freed from feeling like a failure when things are not finished, and hopeful that they will be as my journey comes to its end. I want adventure, and this reminds me I am living in it. Life is not a problem to be solved; it is an adventure to be lived.

I've written down many other thoughts and images over the years, but they couldn't possibly make sense to you. I will spare you the equivalent of looking at my home movies; I fear I have indulged myself already. But let me share one last image, captured in two words: *the meadowlark.*

- *The meadowlark.* The meadowlark has long been my favorite songbird. I suppose to many people it's a simple bird, not really all that colorful, none too spectacular in flight. But I love its song because it evokes so many summer days out in the fields and streams of the West. Because of my story, there is much romance for me in the meadowlark. Its song *means* summer, hay meadows, long lazy days, fly-fishing. More than anything else, it has become for me a symbol of hope. The meadowlark returns to Colorado in the early spring, and as I've mentioned, that typically means it arrives about the same time our major snowstorms hit. What courage; I'm sure if it were me, I'd wait until June when the weather warms up. But they come in spite of the snow, and take their place on fence posts and the tops of small trees, and begin singing. Hearing a midsummer song almost seems out of place when the flurries are whipping about your face. But that is exactly when we need it.

I heard two meadowlarks again this spring, calling and responding to each other on a cold and windy day. God began to speak through them. I heard him urging me to keep my own summer song, even though life's winter tries to throw into my spring cold wind and snow. *Do not throw away your confidence,* he said. *Do not budge from your perch, but sing your song, summer confident, sure of my great goodness toward you. You did not bring this spring, dear child; you do not have to arrange for the summer to follow. They come from thy Father's will, and they will come.* I thought of C. S. Lewis's essay, "The Grand Miracle," where he says,

> To be sure, it feels wintry enough still: but often in the very early spring it feels like that . . . the spring comes down slowly down this way; but the great thing is that the corner has been turned. There is, of course, this difference, that in the natural spring the crocus cannot choose whether it will respond or not. We can. We have the power either of withstanding the spring, and sinking back into the cosmic winter, or of going on into these "high mid-summer pomps" in which our leader, the Son of Man, already dwells, and to which he is calling us. It remains with us to follow or not, to die in this winter, or to go on into that spring and that summer.

Brent was buried on a Thursday afternoon. As we gathered by the graveside, his family and friends, Craig read these words: "I am the resurrection and the life. He who believes in me will live, even though he dies; and whoever lives and believes in me will never die" (John 11:25–26 NIV). He closed his Bible, and we all stood in silence, not really knowing what to say or do; no one wanted to leave; no one really wanted to stay. It seemed so final. At that moment, a meadowlark sang.

This is my song in return.

About the Author

John Eldredge is the founder and director of Ransomed Heart™ Ministries in Colorado Springs, Colorado, a fellowship devoted to helping people recover and live from their deep heart. John is the author of numerous books, including, *Waking the Dead, Wild at Heart, The Sacred Romance*, and *The Journey of Desire*. John lives in Colorado with his wife, Stasi, and their three sons, Samuel, Blaine, and Luke. He is an avid outdoorsman who loves being in the wild.

To learn more about John's seminars, audiotapes, and other resources for the heart, visit him on the Web at: www.RansomedHeart.com

Or write:

Ransomed Heart™ Ministries

P.O. Box 51065

Colorado Springs, CO 80949-1065

Also by John Eldredge

The Journey of Desire Journal and Guidebook
John Eldredge, with Craig McConnell, offers a unique, thought-provoking, and life-recapturing work-book, which invites you to rediscover your God-given desire and to search again for the life you once dreamed of. Less of a workbook and more of a flowing journal, this book includes personal responses to questions from John and Craig. **ISBN 0-7852-6640-2**

Dare to Desire
Complete with beautiful, full-color design, *Dare to Desire* is the perfect book if you are ready to move beyond the daily grind to a life overflowing with adventure, beauty, and a God who loves you more pas-sionately than you dared imagine. With brand-new content as well as concepts from *The Sacred Romance, The Journey of Desire*, and *Wild at Heart*, John Eldredge takes you on a majestic journey through the uncharted waters of the human heart. **ISBN 0-8499-9591-4**

Wild at Heart: A Band of Brothers.
Five friends. Eight days. No scripts. Here's what it looks like to live the message of *Wild at Heart* in a band of real brothers. John and his band of brothers spent eight days shooting this series on a ranch in Colorado. Horses. Rappelling, Whitewater rafting. Fly-fishing. And some of the most honest conversa-tion you will ever hear from men. This is not a scripted instructional video. It is real life and conversation shared with the cameras rolling. If you're looking for more, this is the next step in the *Wild at Heart* adven-ture for you and your band of brothers. The Multi-Media Facilitator's Kit includes John's best-selling *Wild at Heart* hardcover book; the *Wild at Heart Field Manual*; the *Wild at Heart Facilitator's Guide*; the video teaching series available either in VHS or DVD format; and a media kit to help you get the word out so others can join your band of brothers. **VHS—ISBN 1-4002-0087-3 • DVD—ISBN 1-4002-0086-5**

Wild at Heart

Every man was once a boy. And every little boy has dreams, big dreams. But what happens to those dreams when they grow up? In *Wild at Heart*, John Eldredge invites men to recover their masculine heart, defined in the image of a passionate God. And he invites women to discover the secret of a man's soul and to delight in the strength and wildness men were created to offer.

Hardcover—ISBN 0-7852-6883-9 • Abridged Audio in 3 CDs—ISBN 0-7852-6298-9

Abridged Audio in 2 cassettes—ISBN 0-7852-6498-1 • Spanish Edition (*Salvaje de Corazón*)—ISBN 0-8811-3716-2

Wild at Heart Field Manual

Abandoning the format of workbooks-as-you-know-them, the *Wild at Heart Field Manual* will take you on a journey through which you will receive permission to be what God designed you to be—dangerous, passionate, alive, and free. Filled with questions, exercises, personal stories from readers, wide-open writing spaces to record your "field notes," this book will lead you on a journey to discover the masculine heart that God gave you.

ISBN 0-7852-6574-0

AVAILABLE OCTOBER 2003
The Wild at Heart Journal.

This rugged leather-bound guided journey will help men explore their hearts and journal their adventures. This includes totally different material than that found in the *Field Manual*. **ISBN 0-8499-5763-X**

The Sacred Romance

This life-changing book by Brent Curtis and John Eldredge has guided hundreds of thousands of readers from a busyness-based religion to a deeply felt relationship with the God who woos you. As you draw closer to Him, you must choose to let go of other "less-wild lovers," such as perfectionistic drivenness and self-indulgence, and embark on your own journey to recover the lost life of your heart and with it the intimacy, beauty, and adventure of life with God.

Trade Paper Edition—ISBN 0-7852-7342-5 • Special Collector's Edition (Hardcover)—ISBN 0-7852-6723-9

Abridged Audio in 2 Cassettes—ISBN 0-7852-6786-7 • Spanish Edition (*El Sagrado Romance*)—ISBN 0-8811-3648-4

The Sacred Romance Workbook and Journal

John Eldredge offers a guided journey of the heart featuring exercises, journaling, and the arts to usher you into an *experience*—the recovery of your heart and the discovery of your life as part of God's great romance.

ISBN 0-7852-6846-4

The Three Classics:

The Sacred Romance, The Journey of Desire, and *Wild at Heart* are available in one specially priced package. Whether this special set is for yourself, to replace the dog-eared and penciled-in copies you already own, or is a gift to share John's powerful message with someone you love, these *Three Classics from John Eldredge* will continue to give long after they are received. **ISBN 0-7852-6635-6**

Waking the Dead.

In *Waking the Dead*, John Eldredge shows how God restores your heart, your true humanity, and sets you free. There are four streams, Eldredge says, through which you can discover the abundant life: Walking with God, Receiving His Intimate Counsel, Deep Restoration, and Spiritual Warfare. And once the "eyes of your heart" are opened, you will embrace three eternal truths: Things are not what they seem; This is a world at war; and You have a crucial role to play. A battle is raging. And it is a battle for your heart.

Hardcover—ISBN 0-7852-6553-8 • Abridged Audio in 3 CDs—ISBN 0-7852-6299-7

AVAILABLE NOVEMBER 2003
A Guidebook to Waking the Dead: Embracing the Life God Has for You.

In a style similar to *The Journey of Desire Journal and Guidebook*, Eldredge and Craig McConnell lead you on a journey toward a restored heart, true humanity, and ultimate freedom. **ISBN 0-7852-6309-8**